Moon City Review 2010

An Annual
of Poetry, Story, Art, & Criticism

Other Books from Moon City Press

Yankee Doric: America before the Civil War, by Burton Raffel

Morkan's Quarry, by Steve Yates

Some of the Words are Theirs: A Memoir of an Alcoholic Family,
by George H. Jensen, Jr.

Moon City Review 2009: An Annual of Poetry, Story, Art, & Criticism,
edited by Jane Hoogestraat and Lanette Cadle

**Moon City Press titles are distributed through the
University of Arkansas Press:**

<http://www.uapress.com/titles/mcp/mcp.html>

Moon City Review 2010

An Annual
of Poetry, Story, Art, & Criticism

Edited by Lanette Cadle and Marcus Cafagña
Missouri State University

moon city press
springfield missouri
2010

www.mooncitypress.com

Cover Design: Eric Pervukhin

Text Layout: Angelia Northrip-Rivera

Excerpt from *Blue Mars* reprinted with permission of the author

ISBN: 978-0-913785-30-0

Contents

II. Direct from Moon City

III. From Points Beyond

IV. Archival Treasures

LANETTE CADLE

Introduction

For a collection edited by two poets, *Moon City Review 2010: An Annual of Poetry, Story, Art, & Criticism* is heavier on the fiction side, and purposely so. This volume includes writing and art that considers alternate futures, whether dystopic, utopic, fantastic, deluded, or contorted. Although poetry can be a site for speculation, fiction takes the forefront for this genre (or family of genres).

The impetus for the theme, "speculative fictions," is the memory of longtime Missouri State English Department faculty member, Dr. William J. Burling, who passed away this past year. His contribution to literary criticism centering on science fiction remains notable, but for students and faculty who knew him, his excellence in teaching and in writing is a more personal memory. Many current doctorate-holders and candidates can trace the beginnings of their academic success to the rigors encountered in one of Dr. Burling's classes on science fiction.

A current graduate student, Liam Watts contributes a personal essay sharing his memories of Burling the man, the teacher, the scholar. Kim Stanley Robinson shares an excerpt from *Blue Mars*, the third of his acclaimed *Mars* sci-fi trilogy, to give context to Burling's scholarship. And recent M.A. graduate D. Gilson offers an elegiac poem dedicated to Burling the teacher. Many of the pieces in *MCR 2010* could be classed as "speculative fiction," but certainly not all. As we plan to do with future "themed" volumes, we accepted much work outside the theme, simply because it was too good to turn down.

To start things off, *New Arrivals* features four stories that skew a bit off familiar paths. In all four, the universe may seem familiar in the beginning but, somewhere along the way, an alternate world one-door-to-the-left gets constructed, one whose difference is not just to shock or entertain, but to jog expectations, to let readers consider a world tinged with different hues.

At first, this may not seem like "science" fiction. However, science fiction, no matter what label gets applied (and there are many), has two, possibly three main reasons for being, and not all are expressed in every story. The obvious one—to play with and imagine new technologies—is usually a ploy. Granted, stories may be written simply to imagine-into-being new contortions of present machinery, but good science fiction, or speculative fiction if you prefer, is about people: how they live, and how they feel. Most science fiction that gets called literary not only centers on people, it does so in context by carefully constructing future worlds. In other words, it pays close attention to economic and political structures. Kim Stanley Robinson's *Mars* series is an example of this, as the excerpt in this volume demonstrates. Ted Chiles' "Love Under an Invisible Hand" would be another example.

Besides a look at humanity massed across multiple universes like streams of stars, science fiction also takes a close-up view and, by doing so, allows a more personal examination of larger concepts and themes, such as what makes an entity human. Will emotional force be the defining feature in the future? Intelligence? Curiosity? Will humans turn into their own other? Blurred lines and boundaries lead to good speculative writing—of the sort gathered here. "Beauty" by Nancy Gold and "The World to Come" by Pete Duval examine boundaries, as does Juned Subhan's "I See You Clearly," although in a different way.

New Arrivals also features poetry by Jim Daniels, whose latest book, *Having a Little Talk with Capital P Poetry*, was released this year from Carnegie Mellon University Press. We are proud to include his three poems which, while not overtly speculative, definitely have an edge. Another poetry contributor in *New Arrivals*, Jeannine Hall Gailey, is known for her poems that question modern archetypes and play with fantasy.

Not all writers in *MCR 2010* are "names"—yet. In criticism, Missouri State alum Landis Duffett makes a strong contribution. As for creative nonfiction, Missouri State undergraduate Eric Morrow's "The Rise of the Nerd" stands proudly among the works included here; so does the creative nonfiction of Julie Platt, a poet and PhD candidate at yet another MSU (Michigan State), who gives a darkly humorous look at when she "played Indian."

New to this volume (and to succeeding volumes) is the section, *From Points Beyond*, which features translations of work from contemporary writers around the world. Thanks to *MCR* translations editor John Duval and his students from the Programs in Creative Writing and Translation at the University of Arkansas, Fayetteville, *MCR 2010* boasts a strong selection of fiction and poetry, all of which stand very much on their own as literature. The poems by Per Aage Brandt include the original Danish but, given space constraints, the fiction translations are printed without their originals. (In the future, we may extend side-by-side translation to fiction, as well.)

When giving thanks for the many hours contributed to this second volume, the first person I must thank is my co-editor, Marcus Cafagña. His depth of experience in creative writing and its publication has been a great comfort and help throughout the publication process. Of course, two editors are not enough to put together a book of this sort. We owe much to many. *MCR 2010* is partially funded by the Missouri

State University College of Arts and Letters and Department of English; many thanks to Dean Cary Adams and the English Department Head, W. D. Blackmon, for their continued support. Editor for Moon City Press James S. Baumlin, as always, has been a strong supporter, encourager, and behind-the-scenes magician.

Also, we are proud to announce that this year *MCR* has three awards which will continue in future volumes. The Missouri State English Society Award is for submissions by current Missouri State students as of the time of submission. This year's winner is D. Gilson for his poem, "The Last Night in Pummill Hall." The Transom Award is for the best work received "over the transom," i.e., unsolicited. The winner for 2010 is Landis Duffett for his critical piece, "Our Digital Future: Nostalgia, Broadcast Television, and the Televisual Sublime." Finally, the Emerging Artist Award is for work by a promising artist at the beginning of his/her career. This award is for solicited or unsolicited work. The winner for 2010 is Julie Platt for her creative nonfiction essay, "When I Played Indian." Congratulations to all three winners; we are grateful to receive and publish work of this caliber.

Additional thanks are needed for production assistant Jennifer Essary, who managed submissions for *MCR 2010* and worked mightily on promotions and mailings for other Moon City Press books, all while completing her first year in the MA program at Missouri State. Angelia Northrip-Rivera, Senior Instructor in English, once again did the text layout, while Eric Pervukhin contributed the cover art and design (including the unique font of his own making).

The staff of Meyer Library's Special Collections and Archives—David Richards, Anne Baker, and Tracie Gieselman-Holthaus—came through for us as usual, providing scanned reproductions and aiding in research. An Assistant Professor of Photography at Missouri State, Jimmie Allen provided most of the images for *Archival Treasures*. And David

O'Neill once again gave us open access to his collection of O'Neilliana, for which we express an enduring gratitude.

We thank the creative writing faculty at Missouri State University for encouraging students to submit, giving special thanks to those faculty who stepped in to read work when submissions were from past or current students of the editors/readers. We also thank the authors and artists who accepted our invitation to contribute, allowing us once again to offer a volume featuring writers whose differing levels of experience belie the overall excellence of their collective work.

Finally, many thanks are due to the graduate student readers who gave their time to painstakingly read all of the submissions. Readers D. Gilson (poetry), Ben Bogart (fiction), and Heather Cook (creative nonfiction) were joined by *MCR* publications assistant Jennifer Essary and past *MCR* assistant Isaiah Vianese. There was a lot of writing talent seated at that table; more importantly, they used their reading and writing talents humbly, approaching each piece as if it were the first of the day and expecting good things each time.

The first volume in this series gave a history for the name, Moon City. In this second volume dedicated to speculation, future science, and "what if," I will give the myth.

Once again, I take the reader back to the 1870s—back to those early railroad-building years, which saw this raw and beautiful country we call the Ozarks move from a land that measured distances by how far a stagecoach could travel before changing horses to the brink of the modern era, when you could buy a train (and, soon enough, a plane) ticket to literally anywhere.

Springfieldians looked that future square in the face and refused to believe it. Ozark skepticism—an intensified version of Missouri's "Show Me" attitude—this time had some basis in fact. By 1870, there had been more than one failed attempt to finance a railway, with one company mocked in print as having "as much ability to build a railroad to the moon as to Springfield" (Moser).[1] So, when the company that eventually did build that railroad came to town, the city fathers didn't get out the tar and feathers, but they were more than ready to enforce an old contract "to the letter." Faced with a town that refused to "pay extra" for placing a depot near its town square, the railroad company simply moved further north and built a new city—North Springfield—whose original boundary is marked to this day by Division Street. The old Springfieldians had another name for this upstart of a company town that, in their view, existed simply because the tracks were laid there. They called it Moon City, mindful of the old newspaper taunt and dismissive of its chances for success.

But it's all Springfield now—north and south, old and new—and which side won is moot. As Jane Hoogestraat and James S. Baumlin point out in the first volume of *MCR*,

> Whether as a town or as a text, "Moon City" has always been an improvisation. It was, and it remains, a convenient fiction—an invention of entrepreneurs, a flight of fancy, a slap in the face of "old town" expectations, an upstart, Ozarks-style declaration. In its status as a literary-artistic annual (and as an academic small press of the same name), Moon City remains a mythic place, forever a "new town." Like the first railroad, it citifies an early pioneer settlement, bringing in fresh blood. Moon City remains a "place" (a press, a book annual) where Ozarks history and literary-artistic culture can be both remembered and reconstructed, engaging back-and-forth with the rest (and best) of the world "out there," bringing new-

---

[1] Quoted from Arthur Paul Moser's unpublished typescript, "A Brief History of North Springfield Known as 'Moon City'" (1985), which resides in the Local History Department of The Library Center for Springfield-Greene County.

comers in, sending our own out and abroad, all in-terconnected—incorporated, as it were—through mutual interests in poetry, story, art, and criticism.

Welcome to Moon City—again. Let's make this a habit.

Remembering Dr. Burling
(1949–2009)

LIAM R. WATTS

Martian Justice:
A Student's Recollections of Dr. William J. Burling

Overture

On my desk is a motley stack of spiral-bound notebooks. Some have loose pages sticking out of them; each is a different color, and all show various stages of wear. They are the record of courses I took with Dr. William J. Burling (1949–2009) at Missouri State University. Being a seasoned note-taker, I was as good as his amanuensis in class. Once, Burling called me a "colleague." Though an offhand remark, he said it sincerely and later demonstrated its sincerity in both word and deed; it remains the greatest compliment I have ever received. So, what follows is a student's recollections of a man, of his work, of his life as it was parsed and filtered to me, and of the life-experiences that influenced the kind of scholar he became.

Clearly, Burling was a literary Marxist in every aspect of his life's work. He *professed* Marxism, meaning that he lived it, and he was able to teach it *because* he lived it. To readers who dislike or mistrust the Marxist approach to literature, I can only advise you to skim lightly other parts of this essay and go straight to Kim Stanley Robinson, whose *Blue Mars* excerpt shows (rather than tells) the issues behind the critical stance that Burling highlighted in his scholarship. As for *this* essay, I present "what Burling said" and give tribute to a man who based his life's work on principles rather than on popularity.

Setting the Stage

It is 2010 as I write this essay, a decade into the century favored by science fiction authors for that mystical "21st century" description. We now *live* in the future, benefited by technology and advancements that were considered SF a mere generation ago—that were not even imaginable a century ago. In innumerable ways, humanity has advanced to the point where we would seem an alien race—visitors from another world—were we to travel back and visit ourselves in the past. As the Walt Disney World attraction, "The Carousel of Progress," promises: "There's a great big beautiful tomorrow, shining at the end of every day!" And yet, if one pays attention, it's not difficult to notice the worn stitching and fading paint covering the animatronic character who, singing through a permanent smile, proclaims his Disneyan paean of progress.

Our world remains plagued by cultural and ideological strife rooted in tribal differences that have justified countless deaths since the Middle Ages and, indeed, long before. Millions still live in abject poverty, dying of starvation. Throughout the world, women are still treated as property, as chattel with no benefit of civil rights or social justice. Diseases that could have been wiped out by vaccination still have toeholds—and not just in developing nations: they are making come-backs in the modern world, thanks to a mistrust of the very scientific method that has allowed the West to live in modern comfort and material excess.

As I write this essay, the largest man-made disaster ever to affect the ecosphere is playing out in the Gulf of Mexico—a disaster that could devastate and destroy a swath of natural ecology, as well as human habitat and livelihoods, for the foreseeable future. It is a disaster caused by humanity's dependence on a fuel source decidedly *not* futuristic, one belonging to an age in which industry and technology (as we know it) began.

The world we live in today is marked and marred by contradictions. In the simplest of job descriptions, it's the task of the SF author to recognize, unmask, and dramatize these contradictions; and it's the job of the critical scholar to aid in this unmasking. Both the SF author and the critical scholar call attention to culture's ideological blind spots, showing us what we may be missing.

Kim Stanley Robinson is just such an SF author and Burling was just such a scholar. In 2005, Burling began work on the critical anthology, *Kim Stanley Robinson Maps the Unimaginable*. The anthology brings together the essays of many scholars addressing the range of Robinson's fiction. Burling included one of his own essays (originally published in the journal *Utopian Studies*), entitled, "The Theoretical Foundation of Utopian Radical Democracy in *Blue Mars*." I had not yet met Burling when he'd written that essay, but I had the experience, as a graduate student, of studying under him for the four years that he constructed the anthology. During that time, I gained some insight into what drew him to Robinson's work.

If a Gun is Shown in Act I . . . .

Kim Stanley Robinson has a doctorate in English; he is an avid mountain climber and an eco-activist. More important for our purposes, he is a Nebula and Hugo Award winner for his Mars Trilogy: *Red Mars*, *Green Mars*, and *Blue Mars*— the epic story of the colonization and transformation of Mars into a new home for humanity. Robinson is known as a Utopian author, although what that means, according to Robinson, has changed over time. The 2009 Public Affairs Conference at Missouri State University—titled "Sustainable

Actions for a Sustainable Future"—featured Robinson as one of its invited speakers. During his talk, he addressed the issue: when he started writing Utopian fiction, the task was to imagine a perfect society, "and now, thirty years later, I write about worlds in which *we managed to survive* and I'm *still* called a 'Utopian writer.' The definition of 'utopia' has taken a huge downgrade during this last thirty years."

Burling first brought him to my attention in October 2006, introducing Robinson to the class as an SF writer of note who had a compelling social outlook. Burling pointed him out to me in particular, because of Robinson's own scholarship on SF author Philip K. Dick (who was the subject of my own research), and to the class in general as an example of the good that can come when a researcher takes the opportunity to contact another scholar (or a producer of scholarship-worthy material). That is, Burling had himself taken opportunity to contact Robinson regarding the essay he was writing on *Blue Mars*. Out of that contact emerged not just a book project but a growing friendship.

As a variety of science fiction, Utopian fiction brings with it a capacity to unmask contradictions. In his *Critical Theory and Science Fiction* (which Burling used as a text in his SF and Utopian genre classes), Carl Freedman examined SF's qualities as a form of literature and declared it to have a privileged ability to examine the contemporary world as it is: examining society and identifying its issues and problems, SF then points a critical lens at them through the technique of "cognitive estrangement," which removes a situation in time and/or space—thus providing a critical distance. This way of examining the present through an historical, material outlook is, to be forthright, ideological.

But then, as Robinson said at the 2009 Missouri State University Public Affairs Conference, we *all* see the world through the lens of an ideology—the catch is that we rarely see our own lens and are used to proclaiming *other* peoples' lenses as "false consciousness" or ideological. Burling would agree with this assessment, and taught that an ideology tried to make itself invisible—as if it did not exist—to those who live within it. This invisibility trick was the way in which those in power and had the most to gain (economically, politically, militarily) could continue to do so; after all, the predominant ideology would be treated as the *natural* way of things—a reflection of "common sense."

The lens Burling saw through, the one he used as he read and analyzed *Blue Mars*, the one he taught his classes in the final years that I knew him, was *not* the same lens he used growing up. In those early years in northern Wisconsin, he encountered the world through the same ideology that most of us growing up in modern America are taught. However, as he would tell students, the changes he saw in his home-town (and middle America in general) during the 1960s and 1970s were troubling trends that seemed to contradict what he was taught to believe about society, economy, politics. The way factories would pack up and leave for another country, to the economic detriment of the communities they left behind, hinted at changes he couldn't yet grasp. Burling would say that it took him years only *to begin* to understand a different ideology, one that revealed these contradictions to be part of the progression of modern capitalism as it evolved into global-market capitalism.

The hallmark of global-market capitalism is the multi-national or trans-national corporation. In Robinson's *Mars* novels, the "transnats" and "metanationals" directly control the Earth's governments and are responsible for manipulating the development and politics of the burgeoning Martian settlements. In our contemporary world situation, the oil catastrophe that threatens the ecology in and around the Gulf of Mexico is the responsibility of a British corporation working in conjunction with American corporations to pull natural resources out of international waters. Burling would likely have used this event as an illustration of the way global-market capitalism transcends any social or political boundary that, decades earlier, would have constrained the actions of any corporate identity. He would have reminded us that BP once stood for "British Petroleum" and that U. S. Steel was, at one time, *not* an ironic name. Today, national boundaries and identities have become meaningless in corporate terms.

The current state of transnational corporatism was often a subject of Burling's classroom lectures, and it is a significant subject in his analysis of *Blue Mars*. In his essay, Burling summarizes the outcome of the revolution waged by the Martians—as the transplanted humans (the "issei") and the next generation of natives (the "nisei") came to be called—resulting in the expulsion of Earth's governmental representatives:

> The Martians, therefore, have not thrown off a ty-rannical system of rule, but rather have responded to what they see as undue excesses on the part of the powerful Terran meta-national corporations that attempt to impose their will in insensitive and inappropriate ways. (159)

Both Robinson and Burling agree that the "insensitive and inappropriate ways" of corporations go hand-in-hand with the lack of social justice in the world, contributing to the contradictions of our global community and to the violence they do, both to the ecosystem and to human society generally. Burling would often bring up the subject of animal rights (occasionally in conjunction with his daughter's veterinary studies), ecological justice, and gender equality. And he made social justice a key topic in his analysis of *Blue Mars*. Burling acknowledges Robinson's proposal to create social justice by limiting the power of any one group—even the power of commerce and the demands of labor over peoples' lives. The Martian "Dorsa Brevia," a sort of combination of the American Bill of Rights and the British Magna Carta, eventually evolves into a planet-wide democracy, in which the government is decentralized, is made up of obligatorily temporary non-professional politicians, and involves complex spiderwebs of checks-and-balances (166). In this way, the society in Robinson's Martian Utopia develops an entirely new relationship with governmental and economic power—and, perhaps most importantly, a new relationship with the planet and the ecosystem.

Burling shows pointed interest in the Martian legal structure, a dual judiciary system that becomes the most powerful component of government. And the most potent part of the judiciary is the "Environmental Court," which represents and protects the interests of the planet, itself (163). After all, it is the planet that provides life and vital resources—it is as unthinkable, in Robinson's Martian society, to treat the planet *without* justice, care, and consideration as it is to treat fellow humans inhumanely.

The 2009 Public Affairs Conference took place after Burling's passing, so Robinson could speak only in his colleague's memory. But as Robinson said, "Even if this were not a memorial to Bill Burling, I would want to bring up the social justice aspects [of devaluing the future through damaging the ecosystem]." The problems of ecological damage, the lack of social justice around the world, and economic exploitation are an intertwined trifecta of related problems and, in every class I had with Burling, this was made evident. He often spoke about the addiction to mass consumption that is endemic in our culture's ideology, and how this ideology blinds us to the toll our addiction to cheap, disposable commodities takes on the natural resources and on the people who make them. Burling would tell us of his parents and the "Walmart in the attic" they accumulated, allowing them immediately to replace a broken or worn appliance in the house below with a new one stored above. He mentioned that his mother found this quirk humorous, and so did he, but "for very different reasons."

Burling would teach that, in order to examine the problems with culture and ideology, one must examine the *history* of a society—the history of its politics, its social norms, and its art. Before taking up Utopian fiction and SF, perhaps even before fully embracing the critical theories that brought him to his understanding of our late-postmodern world, Burling investigated a different art-form altogether. He is quoted in *Contemporary Authors*:

> After attempting, during the seventies, to write poetry and fiction in Wisconsin, I discovered at Penn State the pleasures of scholarly research and writing. I had originally planned to specialize in twentieth-century American literature when Professor Robert D. Hume introduced me to the possibilities of the London stage of the seventeenth and eighteenth centuries. (55)

His admiration of his thesis advisor, Dr. Robert D. Hume, Evan Pugh Professor of English Literature at Penn State University, was obvious in the way Burling modeled his own scholarship after him. A doctoral student of Hume's at Penn State in the early 80s, Burling earned his PhD in 1985, and Hume's influence led him to research the London theatre with tenacity, resulting in some painstakingly researched books.

The introduction to Burling's *Checklist of New Plays and Entertainments on the London Stage, 1700–1737* describes his manner of acquiring and evaluating material, including the examination of thirty-seven years' worth of eighteenth-century plays for references to *other* dramatic works, countless newspaper articles and advertisements, and even songbooks of the day, all to reconstruct the activities of the London stage (11). His *Summer Theatre in London, 1661–1820, and the Rise of the Haymarket Theatre* is filled with tables of performance dates, monthly box office receipt reports, and the available names of every person who worked in the Haymarket Theatre for each run—down to the individual dressers and machinists.

Naturally, I had to wonder whether Burling embraced materialist-Marxist Critical Theory early on, or simply began with an interest in, and a savvy perception of, the material interactions of society and the labor of forgotten individuals in the production of culture. His first degree was a BS in Psychology from the University of Wisconsin-Eau Claire. This certainly gave background to Burling's significant interest in the psychoanalytical literary theory of Jacques Lacan and to Lacan's equally insightful (and inscrutable) disciple, Slavoj Žižek. For insight in this regard, I took a page from Burling's own book and contacted his old mentor, Professor Hume. As Hume informed me, "I suspect that the grounding in materialist scholarship (books, historical records, manuscripts) was probably the jumping-off point for Bill's move towards Marxist thinking, which (so far as I am aware) developed mostly as he moved into SF and experimental fiction in much more recent periods." Evidently, being so invested and en-wrapped in the research of the historical production of art and the labor involved in its production, he was became more keenly aware of the way commodities (including art) are produced and consumed *today*. Burling's oft-repeated motto, to be asked of any and all cultural production from jeans to poems, was: "Who uses it and what is it for?"

With so much of his life and career invested in the study of literature, one of Burling's most fervent predictions was that one day, in the not-too-distant future, literary study as we know it would come to an end. "Literature," Burling would say, was a "power-play" term used by intellectuals to determine who had "cultural capital" and who was a "cultural peasant." Burling would tease his class, asking who in the world (aside from teachers, whose job it is to dole out cultural capital) still reads Chaucer or *Paradise Lost* or (heresy of heresies!) Shakespeare for any reason other than to be able to say they've done so? Such reading would thus serve as a secret handshake to other intellectuals, declaring that you, too, are worthy to "come and go, / Talking of Michelangelo." The capitalist educational system, from the university down to the grade schools (from which he had removed his daughter to home-school since, as he said, it was obvious that the school system sought to create automatons with permanent smiles), was to continue to separate people, not just by economic class, but by cultural class as well. The belief that literature, or art in general, somehow contained a universal revelation of "the good, the true, and the beautiful" was a delusion—the product of a cultural hegemony. And "literature," so-called, was simply another product, a commodity, that would one day find itself reduced to a relatively minor component of cultural studies.

Burling was a lauded and brilliant scholar who could have found himself at home among the intelligentsia; but he was a populist, a radical. Ruffling feathers, he challenged authority—and challenged his *students* to dare to see the lens through which they themselves examined the world. It's not surprising that science fiction, that genre of vulgar distraction that exists in a literary ghetto, would be where Burling eventually found his scholarly home.

The Curtain Falls

Referring to today's world conditions, Burling wrote in his article on *Blue Mars*, "Numerous challenges exist, such as the ever-expanding profit-driven interests of trans-national capi-

talism and the lack of a mechanism for corporate account-
ability at all levels" (167). Thinking about that, I look again at
news websites depicting the ever-widening Gulf of Mexico
disaster, and I consider the occluded path that the demand
for oil-based products creates from me on back through the
stores that stock products in bulk, factories that make plastic
products, refineries that process petroleum, the ripping of
this resource out of the ground, and the effect all this has
on the planet—and all the people all over the world who are
involved in the path from earth to me.

Burling taught me to consider this path and the spider-
web of interaction along it. He taught that SF was a form of
artistic production that is uniquely suited to exploring the
material interactions between society and what its produc-
tions. It often explores the issues and the contradictions and
points out the problems. But Utopian fictions, like *Blue Mars*,
go a step further: they "contribute in very real ways to the
process of struggle by simply envisioning theoretical political alternatives" (167). The essential message of "The Theoretical Foundation of Utopian Radical Democracy in *Blue
Mars*" is that it is possible to think beyond the fundamental problems of our world, beyond the very *sources* of those
problems; and that's precisely what Kim Stanley Robinson
has done. Robinson has pinpointed the roots of our society's
political, economic, social, and environmental problems and
extrapolated out to how bad they can get, and then imagines
an attainable solution based on social and ecological justice.

Please Watch Your Step as You Leave

I have re-shelved relevant books, filed away photocopied
pages, and archived electronic files. The class notebooks remain on my desk. The act of poring over each page of my
notes was a bitter-sweet journey as I read passages that re-

minded me of how much a person's world can change in such a short time. The student who began scrawling in barely legible ink the words of a curious man with a shock of gray hair and a piercing gaze, was a very different one from the one who wrote in a notebook years later, "Pre-capitalist storytelling was communal; the bourgeois novel is isolated!" I think about how little idea I had that my final note in the book at the bottom of the stack would be the last words I'd hear by the man whom I referred to as my "mentor," and who once called me his "colleague."

As Anton Chekhov wrote, "Knowledge is of no value unless you put it into practice." Theory put into practice: *praxis*. I wonder if I have the wisdom, the skill, or the principles to put into action the knowledge I have recorded—to embrace praxis. Burling often said that, in order to have anything worth saying, you must have a theory, and you must have a model. I have a stack of notebooks that may represent both—and a blinking cursor on my computer screen, inviting me to write.

Works Cited

Burling, William J. *A Checklist of New Plays and Entertainments on the London Stage, 1700–1737*. Cranbury, N.J.: Associated University Presses, 1993. Print.

———. "The Theoretical Foundation of Utopian Radical Democracy in *Blue Mars.*" *Kim Stanley Robinson Maps the Unimaginable: Critical Essays*. Ed. William J. Burling. Vol. 13 of *Critical Explorations in Science Fiction and Fantasy*. Ed. Donald E. Palumbo and C.W. Sullivan III. North Carolina: McFarland & Co., 2009. Print.

———. *Summer Theatre in London, 1661–1820, and the Rise of the Haymarket Theatre*. Madison, N.J.: Fairleigh Dickinson University Press, 2000. Print.

"Burling, William J." *Contemporary Authors. New Revision Series*. Detroit: Gale Research Co., 1981. Print.

Freedman, Carl Howard. *Critical Theory and Science Fiction*. Hanover: Wesleyan University Press, 2000. Print.

Hume, Robert D. Personal e-mail to Liam R. Watts. 20 May 2010.

Robinson, Kim Stanley. *Blue Mars*. New York: Bantam, 1997. Print.

———. "Climate Change and the Pursuit of Happiness." Sustainable Actions for a Sustainable Future. 2009 Public Affairs Conference, Missouri State University, Springfield, MO. 22 Apr. 2009. Address.

KIM STANLEY ROBINSON

Excerpt from *Blue Mars*

Unnumbered chapter from "Part Three: A New Constitution"

So he went back to the big table, ready to tackle the next-worst problem. That brought him back to earth again. There were a hundred next-worst problems, all small until you actually took them on, at which point they became insoluble. In all the squabbling it was very hard to see any signs of growing accord. In some areas, in fact, it seemed to be getting worse. The middle points of the Dorsa Brevia document were causing trouble; the more people considered them, the more radical they became. Many around the table clearly believed that Vlad and Marina's eco-economic system, while it had worked for the underground, was not something that should be codified in the constitution. Some complained because it impinged on local autonomy, others because they had more faith in traditional capitalist economics than in any new system. Antar spoke often for this last group, with Jackie sitting right next to him, obviously in support. This along with his ties to the Arab community gave his statements a kind of double weight, and people listened. "This new economy that's being proposed," he declared one day at the table of tables, repeating his theme, "is a radical and unprecedented intrusion of government into business."

Suddenly Vlad Taneev stood up. Startled, Antar stopped speaking and looked over.

Vlad glared at him. Stooped, massive-headed, shaggy-eyebrowed, Vlad rarely if ever spoke in public; he hadn't said a thing in the congress so far. Slowly the greater part of the warehouse went silent, watching him. Art felt a quiver of anticipation; of all the brilliant minds of the First Hundred, Vlad was perhaps the most brilliant—and, except for Hiroko, the most enigmatic. Old when they had left Earth, intensely private, Vlad had built the Acheron labs early on and stayed there as much as possible thereafter, living in seclusion with Ursula Kohl and Marina Tokareva, two more of the great first ones. No one knew anything for certain about the three of them, they were a limit-case illustration of the insular nature of other people's relationships; but this of course did not stop gossip, on the contrary, people talked about them all the time, saying that Marina and Ursula were the real couple, that Vlad was a kind of friend, or pet; or that Ursula had done most of the work on the longevity treatment, and Marina most of the work on eco-economics; or that they were a perfectly balanced equilateral triangle, collaborating on all that emerged from Acheron; or that Vlad was a bigamist of sorts who used two wives as fronts for his work in the separate fields of biology and economics. But no one knew for sure, for none of the three ever said a word about it.

Watching him stand there at the table, however, one had to suspect that the theory about him being just a front man was wrong. He was looking around in a fiercely intent, slow glare, capturing them all before he turned his eye again on Antar.

"What you said about government and business is absurd," he stated coldly. It was a tone of voice that had not been heard much at the congress so far, contemptuous and dismissive. "Governments always regulate the kinds of business they allow. Economics is a legal matter, a system of laws. So far, we have been saying in the Martian underground that as a matter of law, democracy and self-government are the innate rights of every person, and that these rights are not to be suspended when a person goes to work. You"—he waved a hand to indicate he did not know Antar's name— "do you believe in democracy and self-rule?"

"Yes!" Antar said defensively.

"Do you believe in democracy and self-rule as the fundamental values that

government ought to encourage?"

"Yes!" Antar repeated, looking more and more annoyed.

"Very well. If democracy and self-rule are the fundamentals, then why should people give up these rights when they enter their workplace? In politics we fight like tigers for freedom, for the right to elect our leaders, for freedom of movement, choice of residence, choice of what work to pursue—control of our lives, in short. And then we wake up in the morning and go to work, and all those rights disappear. We no longer insist on them. And so for most of the day we return to feudalism. That is what capitalism is—a version of feudalism in which capital replaces land, and business leaders replace kings. But the hierarchy remains. And so we still hand over our lives' labor, under duress, to feed rulers who do no real work."

"Business leaders work," Antar said sharply. "And they take the financial risks—"

"The so-called risk of the capitalist is merely one of the privileges of capital."

"Management—"

"Yes yes. Don't interrupt me. Management is a real thing, a technical matter. But it can be controlled by labor just as well as by capital. Capital itself is simply the useful residue of the work of past laborers, and it could belong to everyone as well as to a few. There is no reason why a tiny nobility should own the capital, and everyone else therefore be in service to them. There is no reason they should give us a living wage and take all the rest that we produce. No! The system called capitalist democracy was not really democratic at all. That is why it was able to turn so quickly into the metanational system, in which democracy grew ever weaker and capitalism ever stronger. In which one percent of the population owned half of the wealth, and five percent of the population owned ninety-five percent of the wealth. History has shown which values were real in that system. And the sad thing is that the injustice and suffering caused by it were not at all necessary, in that the technical means have existed since the eighteenth century to provide the basics of life to all.

"So. We must change. It is time. If self-rule is a fundamental value, if simple justice is a value, then they are values everywhere, including in the workplace where we spend so much of our lives. That was what was said in point four of the Dorsa Brevia agreement. It says everyone's work is their own, and the worth of it cannot be taken away. It says that the various modes of production belong to those who created them, and to the common good of the future generations. It says that the world is something we all steward together. That is what it says. And in our years on Mars, we have developed an economic system that can keep all those promises. That has been our work these last fifty years. In the system we have developed, all economic enterprises are to be small cooperatives, owned by their workers and by no one else. They hire their management, or manage themselves. Industry guilds and co-op associations will form the larger structures necessary to regulate trade and the market, share capital, and create credit."

Antar said scornfully, "These are nothing but ideas. It is utopianism and nothing more."

"Not at all." Again Vlad waved him away. "The system is based on models from Terran history, and its various parts have all been tested on both worlds, and have succeeded very well. You don't know about this partly because you are ignorant, and partly because metanationalism itself steadfastly ignored and denied all alternatives to it. But most of our microeconomy has been in successful operation for centuries in the Mondragon region of Spain. The different parts of the macroeconomy have been used in the pseudo-metanat Praxis, in Switzerland, in India's state of Kerala, in Bhutan, in Bologna Italy, and in many other places, including the Martian underground itself. These organizations were the precursors to our economy, which will be democratic in a way capitalism never even tried to be."

A synthesis of systems. And Vladimir Taneev was a very great synthesist; it was said that all the components of the longevity treatment had already been there, for instance, and that Vlad and Ursula had simply put them together. Now in his economic work with Marina he was claiming to have done the same kind of thing. And although he had not mentioned the longevity treatment in this discussion, nevertheless it lay there like the table itself, a big cobbled-together achievement, part of everyone's lives. Art looked around and thought he could see people thinking, well, he did it once in biology and it worked; could economics be more difficult?

Against this unspoken thought, this unthought feeling, Antar's objections did not seem like much. Metanational capitalism's track record at this point did little to support it; in the last century it had precipitated a massive war, chewed up the Earth, and torn its societies apart. Why should they not try something new, given that record?

Someone from Hiranyagarba stood and made an objection from the opposite direction, noting that they seemed to be abandoning the gift economy by which the Mars underground had lived.

Vlad shook his head impatiently. "I believe in the underground economy, I assure you, but it has always been a mixed economy. Pure gift exchange coexisted with a monetary exchange, in which neoclassical market rationality, that is to say the profit mechanism, was bracketed and contained by society to direct it to serve higher values, such as justice and freedom. Economic rationality is simply not the highest value. It is a tool to calculate costs and benefits, only one part of a larger equation concerning human welfare. The larger equation is called a mixed economy, and that is what we are constructing here. We are proposing a complex system, with public and private spheres of economic activity. It may be that we ask people to give, throughout their lives, about a year of their work to the public good, as in Switzerland's national service. That labor pool, plus taxes on private co-ops for use of the land and its resources, will enable us to guarantee the so-called social rights we have been discussing—housing, health care, food, education—things that should not be at the mercy of market rationality. Because *la salute non si paga,* as the Italian workers used to say. Health is not for sale!"

This was especially important to Vlad, Art could see. Which made sense—for in the metanational order, health most certainly had been for sale, not only medical care and food and housing, but preeminently the longevity treatment itself, which so far had been going only to those who could afford it. Vlad's greatest invention, in other words, had become the property of the privileged, the ultimate class distinction—long life or early death—a physicalization of class that almost resembled divergent species. No wonder he was angry; no wonder he had turned all his efforts to devising an economic system that would transform the longevity treatment from a catastrophic possession to a blessing available to all.

"So nothing will be left to the market," Antar said.

"No no no," Vlad said, waving at Antar more irritably than ever. "The market will always exist. It is the mechanism by which things and services are exchanged. Competition to provide the best product at the best price, this is inevitable and healthy. But on Mars it will be directed by society in a more active way. There will be not-for-profit status to vital life-support matters, and then the freest part of the market will be directed away from the basics of existence toward nonessentials, where venture enterprises can be undertaken by worker-owned co-ops, who will be free to try what they like. When the basics are secured and when the workers own their own businesses, why not? It is the process of creation we are talking about."

Jackie, looking annoyed at Vlad's dismissals of Antar, and perhaps intending to divert the old man, or trip him up, said, "What about the ecological aspects of this economy that you used to emphasize?"

"They are fundamental," Vlad said. "Point three of Dorsa Brevia states that the land, air, and water of Mars belong to no one, that we are the stewards of it for all the future generations. This stewardship will be everyone's responsibility, but in case of conflicts we propose strong environmental courts, perhaps as part of the constitutional court, which will estimate the real and complete environmental costs of economic activities, and help to coordinate plans that impact the environment."

"But this is simply a planned economy!" Antar cried.

"Economies are plans. Capitalism planned just as much as this, and metanationalism tried to plan everything. No, an economy is a plan."

Antar, frustrated and angry, said, "It's simply socialism returned."

Vlad shrugged. "Mars is a new totality. Names from earlier totalities are deceptive. They become little more than theological terms. There are elements one could call socialist in this system, of course. How else remove injustice from economy? But private enterprises will be owned by their workers rather than being nationalized, and this is not socialism, at least not socialism as it was usually attempted on Earth. And all the co-ops are businesses—small democracies devoted to some work of other, all needing capital. There will be a market, there will be capital. But in our system workers will hire capital rather than the other way around. It's more democratic that way, more just. Understand me—we have tried to evaluate each feature of this economy by how well it aids us to reach the goals of more justice and more freedom. And justice and freedom do not contradict each other as much as has been claimed, because freedom in an injust system is no freedom at all. They both emerge together. And so it is not so impossible, really. It is only a matter of enacting a better system, by combining elements that have been tested and shown to work. This is the moment for that. We have been preparing for this opportunity for seventy years. And now that the chance has come, I see no reason to back off just because someone is afraid of some old words. If you have any specific suggestions for improvements, we'll be happy to hear them."

He stared long and hard at Antar. But Antar did not speak; he had no specific suggestions.

The room was filled with a charged silence. It was the first and only time in the congress that one of the issei had stood up and trounced one of the nisei in public debate. Most of the issei liked to take a more subtle line. But now one of the ancient radicals had gotten mad and risen up to smite one of the neoconservative young power mongers—who now looked like they were advocating a new version of an old hierarchy, for purposes of their own. A thought which was conveyed very well indeed by Vlad's long look across the table at Antar, full of disgust at his reactionary selfishness, his cowardice in the face of change. Vlad sat down; Antar was dismissed.

D. GILSON

The Last Night in Pummill Hall

For Bill Burling

I stood on the top floor in the central stairwell,
every empty classroom and office dark, breathing
easy. This could be any condemned building

on any campus in America—these academies
living, growing and outgrowing, shedding skins.
Every box has been packed now, I know, having

packed many of them myself. In goes the Pound
and Eliot, the Post-Colonial theory and linguistic
atlases, Ernest, Emily, Anonymous. They soldier on

and so do we. But what—and who—stays?
I sit atop a step of cracked linoleum, flecked
green and something the color of wheat,

and it wafts—really, it wafts—all around
me. Composition class, freshman year with
a teacher young and smart and (not) least of all

sex, personified. Personification. Or the shadow
of a student. He dropped out, got drafted and shot
dead in Laos. The periods are all falling

into place; a semicolon sleeps lazily and I smell
mold, or the beginning of mold, or the remnants
of mold. A teacher—he taught me social justice,

we tried to deconstruct Alf in light of Capitalism
but he's buried now, having tea with Derrida
and Emma Goldman—he shows them his old

office, these stomping grounds. The building
breathes and I breathe in unison, lay across
that stairwell before calling it all a night.

I. New Arrivals

JIM DANIELS

Cutting My Grandfather's Grass in Detroit

when he could no longer.
Rusty gas can spilling into dust.
Yank yank yanking till it caught.
He squirmed in a metal porch chair in his straw fedora
as if he had to go, as if he had something to say
but—but but but butbutbut.
In his dank basement, all the tools in the world
sat clean and oiled and ready to march
while their leader sat outside in the heat
with a yellow handkerchief.
He kept a skunky beer in his fridge for such occasions.
Back and forth, shooting up the occasional rock
at which he'd nod. Perhaps acknowledging
life's unexpected projectiles.
He pinned a twenty to the inside of his shirt
to elude muggers. If only he'd move.
You can die here if you want,
my father always threatened. He did.

The blade plastered grass against the underside of the mower.
The sweet smell of gas and cut grass created waves
of hallucinatory possibilities there in the middle of Detroit
surrounded by two vacant rubbled lots.
Just one beer, always, with your name on it.
Dandelions and dust, but he wanted it cut.
Perhaps he was sending a message to an obscure saint—
St. Turfinfinger, patron saint of Broken Harps.
He had one in his hallway, donated by the abandoned church

across the street. I choked down the beer.
We talked about a trapeze artist he once knew
or the Proving Grounds at Packard Motors where he tested
a 10,000 cylinder engine and ended up on an abandoned planet
very similar to the very spot on which he sat.

He called me Jimmy, and no one else did.
So the day he called me boy, I knew what patch
of grass he was headed for. Damn it, Boy, he called me.
I wanted the street to know he had a strong young man
looking out for him, more real than the fake dog
he conjured with appropriate signage
and dog house, bones and bowls. When I drove
away, he always waved till I was out of sight,
and I did the same for him.
Ah, gasoline. Ah, cut grass. A small patch,
sneeze of green on the dusty gray street. Two
of his own children had died in that house.
I always missed a spot so it look more
like somebody lived there.

Jim Daniels

Cutwoman in the Corner House

my mother the R.N., the designated secret
sharer for women in flight angling across
the lined square grid of streets built by men

Mrs. Anders climbed the fence to see her
Mrs. Blondell and the glass shard
Mrs. Laney and the teeth, Mrs. Dodge and the burn
my mother held ice against their sobs

if women in trouble emitted contrails
the signals quickly dissipated, wind gusted
dogs howled husbands hammered and cursed
red cross in invisible ink shades yanked down

the ice cream man the sirens the drunken hours
my brothers and sisters pressed against the closed
kitchen door, our father at the factory our TV ignited
for warmth 1960s situations without comedy

the high-pitched alarm only women could hear
at our kitchen table between rounds
what my mother did forever dissipated. All we knew
she patched them up, sent them back out there.

JIM DANIELS

Vomit on the Soccer Field

Stephanie clutches her chest
as vomit splashes onto the muddy grass.

You might want to stop right there. Pick up
your ball and kick it all the way home.
I'm the coach standing next to her,
waving on the other girls to keep playing!
I don't know what's wrong with her
and I don't just mean now. She slurs words slow.
Something missing in her big wild head.
Today, it's her asthma or eating too close to practice.
I'm trying to call somebody to come get her.
Nobody home. Miss Ne-Ne, a jitney driver,
scheduled to pick her up after practice.
We've still got half an hour
to kill. Miss Ne-Ne! I want to call her back
from the moon or whatever planet she's circling
on these city streets, picking up enough to get by.

When Stephanie says she's done, I lead her away
from the puke, sit her on the edge of the track
and return to the others, who are horrified and—
well, no—fascinated, disgusted. Stephanie is not
one of them. Not bright. Not white. Not fast or light.
We scrimmage. The ball never rolls through the puke spot.

After, I stand with Stephanie and my daughter
who helpfully hopefully sees the imaginary silver car
a dozen times. Miss Ne-Ne, Miss Ne-Ne, Stephanie
mumbles into prayer.

Miss Ne-Ne arrives fifteen minutes late.
She leads Stephanie away by the hand
like—like—I can only stare.
The puke spot. That's what they call it,
even next practice when we can see nothing.
Stephanie doesn't return.
What was her story? one girl asks.
Though I'm guessing none of them
really wants to know.

Nancy Gold

Beauty

She woke one morning from uneasy dreams to find that her beauty was missing. She looked on the floor beneath her mirror, thinking it may have slipped from her reflection during the night. Her search revealed nothing but the rug. A small spot marked it, to be sure, but it was only one of those odd spots that develop on carpets, and was much too small besides to be her beauty.

She checked the refrigerator, in case her beauty had been hungry—as her keys sometimes were—to be found sprawled, replete, across a tub of yogurt or cottage cheese. It wasn't there.

A thorough search of her apartment forced her to conclude that perhaps, instead of missing from her reflection, her beauty had left her face. She rested her fingers lightly upon her features. It reminded her of spiders, and she shuddered under her own touch. Careful examination revealed that the tip of her nose leaned slightly to one side, the right nostril was bigger than the left, and her left eye, instead of being almond-shaped, was now most decidedly a square. A comparison in the mirror verified these findings, and in addition, a line of red blotches staggered from her upper lip to the outer corner of her right eye.

She had always known that her beauty would leave someday, but she hadn't thought it would be so soon. Each morning and evening she had smoothed expensive creams over her face, across her forehead, down the slope of her nose that turned up just the right amount at the end, over the swell of her cheekbones, and down the sides of her face, lingering just a moment at the jaw before anointing the delicate skin of her neck.

She had taken such good care of her beauty - why would it leave?

It was Sunday, and she had planned to stay in, work on her bills, and to do a load of laundry. She decided that she would continue her day as planned, and though she had never attempted these tasks without her beauty, they most likely could still be done. She found that they could; indeed, she even managed to put a few things away, and to vacuum the rug.

In the evening she checked her reflection again, hopeful that things had resumed their normal course sometime during the afternoon. But she found that her left eye, in addition to being a perfect square, had also migrated a bit up her face into her forehead, and that her mouth seemed to be growing wider, and its edges now reached almost as far across her face as the outer corners of her eyes. Still, she went to bed that night confident that her beauty would return by morning.

When she awoke the next day she rose slowly from bed, savoring the thought of greeting her beauty. She avoided the mirror - it wouldn't do to act too eager to see it again. She filled a bowl with cereal, careful not to look into her spoon. As a child she had looked into a spoon and had been horrified by the distorted image that appeared to her. She had never really been fond of spoons since then. She successfully avoided the spoon but caught her reflection in her coffee—her beauty had not returned. A boil squatted on her forehead, and her right eye seemed to be sliding closer to her hairline. The middle of her lower lip had split and bulged forth a fleshy redness. Her right nostril had grown so large that it seemed to be pushing the rest of her nose aside. She risked a glance into the spoon, thinking that its distortion might put her reflection right, but it didn't oblige.

She strode to her closet, considered which outfit would best offset the face. Most of her clothes ended up strewn on the floor about her. She felt they were being difficult on purpose. She swept her hand along the shelf of her closet, in case something hid from her, and found a dusty old hat with a large brim. She did not usually wear hats and regarded it with some suspicion. She did not remember how she'd come to have it. But she put it on and examined herself in the mirror. True, it was not at all stylish and probably hadn't been even before the brim had been bent and the bow at the back mashed askew. But it did succeed in covering the boils erupting along her forehead; there were four and a half of them now. That counted for something.

She picked up a black lace skirt and draped it over her face. It looked like her head was covered to take her to a hangman's noose. Sighing, she found a scissors, cut a panel from the skirt, and stapled it along the brim of the hat. It looked awkward. The hat was light blue, the lace deepest black, and her cutting had been uneven, leaving the lace veil to stumble drunkenly along the edge. It came down lower on the left side than the right, but she couldn't be sure that it wasn't her face causing this effect. Still, she could see out, while it was very difficult to see in.

She left her apartment and glanced beneath her windows to see if her beauty were lying there, waiting for her to find it, ready to come home after its little adventure. She was feeling put out by now; the game had gone on long enough. She peered between the Lexuses and Audis and Saabs that lined the curb to no avail.

She walked on to the grocers. People were not as solicitous as she was accustomed to; nobody offered to let her go before them in line, or to carry out her bags. Still, she managed. People did look at her. But except for a small child who

9

peered up into her face from below, and then ran back to his mother, howling and clawing at his eyes, she did not seem to frighten anyone.

On her way home, people followed her with their eyes. She was accustomed to attention, but this was of a different kind. A group of graceless young children pointed to her and asked their mother why she kept her face covered. She turned towards them and tipped her head back slowly, almost but not quite revealing her face, and smiled as they watched, riveted.

She noticed other people who wore hats and wondered if they covered problems worse than her own, misshapen skulls or mangled hair. She laughed to herself, thinking of all of the people she knew who could benefit from wearing hats.

She entered the elevator in her building and was joined by a woman in a luscious cream felt hat. Taffeta circled the brim in twists and waves and dipped into a graceful fall overthe face. The woman below it must be some neighbor of hers; she hadn't paid attention before.

"Hello," she said. "Lovely hat."

"Thank you," the woman replied, and drew up her posture even more erect.

"As you can see, I'm rather in need of a new hat," she said. "Do you know where I might find a good one?"

The woman looked her up and down, stepped closer and raised her fingers to the edge of the black veil, then tilted her head. Even though she could not see the woman's face, she knew that the eyebrows were raised, seeking permission to lift the veil. She nodded once, and the other woman's fingers lifted the fabric slowly. She left it raised for a moment, looked at the face from the left side, the right side, the front. Then she carefully placed the veil back down.

10

"Sofia's," she said, and handed her a card. "Tell her Mrs. Thurber sent you."

Sofia's was not in a part of town she knew. But Mrs. Thurber's hat had been exquisite, exactly along the lines of what she was seeking. It would be worth a trip out of her way. Streets became narrower, the sidewalks less even. The buildings were closer to the road and seemed to be herding her towards the passing cars. A few people were about, but they scurried in and out of the buildings, hardly glancing at her. The address marked a pair of doors graced with worn brass handles that curved outward and slightly away from each other, then came closer again at the bottom. A distorted heart. A small sign on the left said "Sofia's." She sniffed. It was hard to imagine Mrs. Thurber's elegant hat in this neighborhood.

She knocked and walked in. After all, if it were a shop, customers must be welcome to enter. Surrounding her was such a confusion of shapes and colors that at first nothing stood out as a recognizable object. Yellow paisley fabric overlapped a bolt of blue-and-white polka dots, tangles of ribbon straggled over a rack of animal tails - raccoon and fox and hawk. Thread unspooled across the floor, and blocks of wood in different sizes and shapes formed haphazard piles wherever a bit of counter was not occupied by something else. She felt disoriented and lifted her veil to focus more clearly.

"Lost your beauty, eh?"

She dropped the veil and turned, looking for the source of the voice. What she had thought was a pile of discolored fleece moved, and she saw that it was really hair, with a small woman beneath it. All that extended above the counter was the hair, a pair of round, gold-rimmed glasses, and a decidedly bulbous nose. The woman made her way through the disarray.

"Happens to all of us, dearie. Why, just look at me!" the woman cackled.

"Are you Sofia?"

"Yes, dearie. What have you come here for?"

"Mrs. Thurber suggested that I come."

"To get your beauty back?" Sofia asked.

She opened her mouth, then snapped it shut again.

"You look like a fish, dearie. If Mrs. Thurber sent you, I suppose you want a hat. I have done some fine work with her. She was quite stunning, in her day." Sofia started rummaging through the shop, picking up a bit of ribbon here, lace or velvet there. She took a tape from her pocket and began measuring. "I see you in something made of felt. A basic black and white to start, I think."

"My beauty. Is it possible?"

"Why, are you having trouble doing without it? I lost my beauty years ago, and I still manage every day."

"Of course I'm fine."

"I can see that, dearie. Well, you can come back, or wait next door if you like."

She walked outside, turned, and opened the right hand door. It appeared to be some kind of club, with tables and chairs scattered around the space. At one end of the room was an elevated stage. She sat at the back and watched people fill the tables at the front.

The house lights went down and the stage lights came up, revealing a single wooden bar stool flanked by full length mirrors. A hunched-over woman staggered across the stage, each step a battle to balance the sway of her humped back. She climbed up on the stool and faced the audience, baring her teeth in a grimace or a smile.

"Welcome. Welcome all to Club Pulchritude."

Several people in the audience clapped, and the woman waved and nodded, her gray hair catching the light like a halo. Music started, and a spotlight hit her. She swayed slowly on the stool, revealing a little more of her hump at each turn. Then she climbed up on the stool and untied her robe. With her back to the audience she dipped the back of the robe, letting it drop an inch, an inch and a half, then pulling it up again, each time gaining ground until it seemed there could be no more to see, and then she would drop it further still. With a final flourish the music ended and she squatted down sideways on the stool. The robe slithered to the floor. The hump arched over her, dominated her, and naked, it was clear that she could have been formed no other way. The audience clapped wildly. The woman snagged her robe, turned her glorious humped back to the audience, and teasingly recovered herself with the robe, inch by inch. The audience clapped and stomped their feet. Once covered, she cautiously climbed down from the stool and waddled off of the stage.

A second woman came on stage. She walked up to one of the mirrors, primped her hair, winked at her reflection. Then she drew down a zipper on the back of her sweater and shrugged it off her right shoulder. A light came on above the mirror opposite, illuminating another small arm growing from the woman's back. She waved at her reflection in the mirror, and the little arm waved back. They wiggled their fingers at each other. The woman moved to the center of the stage and leaned backwards. The tiny arm wiggled its fingers at the audience, which wiggled theirs in return. Then the arm swept towards her back in a bow.

She stood up, walked backwards out of the room, bile rising in her throat, unable to look away from the stage, feeling her way in the darkness. She pushed through the first door she found, out into the street, and leaned against the wall, the bricks rough against her hands and the sky nearly as dark as the place she'd just left. Drawing a deep breath, she straightened her shoulders and moved away.

A coffee shop, she decided, was just what she needed. Bright lights, everyday people having conversations and drinking coffee. She looked for someone to ask, but the streets were empty. These shops were everywhere; surely if she walked a little ways she would find one.

A few blocks later she heard running footsteps and stepped closer to the buildings. Hands grabbed her from behind, pulled her back into a doorway, ripped her sleeve. Raspy breaths panted in her ear, and the hands pulled her arms together behind her back. The man pushed her up against the door, pressed her there with his body, and she wasn't sure if the rank scent she smelled was him or her own fear, but it filled her, drowning her. He pulled at her coat, at her blouse, spilled buttons onto the ground, shoved his leg roughly between hers.

He tore off her hat and she thrust her face down, away. He grabbed her hair and twisted it back so that her head and her face followed, and she smiled; smiled and smiled until it seemed her face would break, and it did, with the sound of ice cracking across a pond. The light was dim, shadowed by his bulk and the doorway but still he could see, could see her enough. He shoved her away and howled and howled as he ran.

She collapsed onto the ground, flailed around in the darkness for her hat, which she returned it to her head without dusting it off or setting the ribbon aright. She pulled the sides of her coat close around her and staggered to her feet. After three steps she started running, the staccato of her heels echoing off of the empty storefronts and cracked sidewalks, a drum beat urging her on until she saw the two doors with the two brass handles. She stopped. The handles arched back like the curve of a baby's ear. The door above one was marked "Sofia's." The other was warm in her hands.

ALYSSE HOTZ

Tuesday Afternoon

It happens that I am tired of being a woman.
It happens that I go to the record stores and the boutiques
all outside my skin, head full of mirrors, like a funhouse
that twists my belly to the mechanical brim of my face.

The lights in supermarkets make me sob out loud.
I want nothing but a tryst of gladiolas, the slow turning brown.
I want to see no more airplanes, no more refrigerators,
nor beggars, nor police dogs, nor suspension bridges.

It happens that I am tired of my teeth and my nose,
my breasts and silly fingernails.
It happens that I am tired of being a woman.

Just the same it would smell sweet
to scare a child with a dead bird. It would be beautiful
to knock a liquor store clerk into heaven
with the flat edge of a machete. I would laugh
until I no longer breathed.

I do not want to go on being the soil of the earth,
shattered, molten, head crunching underfoot like leaves,
drunks pissing in my hair behind a row of hedges.
The city's trash collects in wastebaskets that burn
when struck with real matches.

I do not want to be the interrogator of so many truths.
I do not want to continue as the signified of speech,
an acorn plucked from branches by a squirrel and dropped
on a car's hood where I only crack and dent.

For this reason, Tuesday blurs through me like wind,
the weight of my body gags at each and every
stop sign. I wield lies the size of guillotines
at any passerby who dares to look me in the eye.

And I'm pulled along to certain intersections, to certain bald-headed
cemeteries, to dives where the women are twice my size,
to certain bookstores that reek of mayonnaise,
to lovely gutters where the smoke rises like perfume.

There are cars the texture of pumpkins, and wonderful knives
strung like tea-lights in the butcher's window.
There are prosthetic legs walking down the sidewalks
without their owners.

There are bicycles and purses, clocks and very ugly trees.
I walk through these streets with face, with legs, with shades
of gray so I can catch the wires in peoples' faces, the blank
of my eyeballs rummaging their bruised-black skies. I swat at them
like flies, cross them over with a hex for smiling
at the park bench, the family eatery, the brick wall
stricken with illegible graffiti.

ALYSSE HOTZ

Resolution

It was the winter of trying.
Even when the streets blurred coffee brown,
aching to close ranks, we failed like liars to impress
our bodies on the still-wet pavement.

I know now why the cold became
our sheets. And why the oven, tired
of our breathing, gave out before the ice
storm in February. The windows

croaked and whistled songs we well knew
while the shutters endured, perfectly
mute, studying the wind's machinery.
Only the floorboards quaked with shame.

This sort of defeat, I think, is my echo
in the dark: venerable, portentous,
rimmed with an appetite for centuries—of late.
It's a well of pessimism and guile

penning letters in green; in the sink
a single plate, the over anxious humming
of the washer. And always, then, the quiet
cold of night. A simplicity not of space

heaters and wool, but of bracing
for the new year, you and me, half-starved,

half-filled with the intent to injure, the resolve
on our tongues turning blue. This winter is for dirty snow.

This winter for the shovel. How you forgive it
like the right words leveled at closed ears,
how we look each other in the eye
and conspire to let the goddamn building freeze.

JUNED SUBHAN

I See You Clearly

For Damien Cheshire

She was the kind of woman who contended that if you were perfect, if you made a genuine effort to be perfect, the chance of anything going wrong was not only impossible, it was unutterable.

That was what Fiona recited to herself, repeatedly, when her car broke down on the road. It was a tarnished orange-brown Shelby Mustang with a caramel-leather interior, which she'd bought second-hand. The salesman had assured Fiona over coffee in his untidy office when she signed all the documents that it was safe to drive and would last her a long time. There was absolutely no problem with it. Unfortunately, it did not have power steering, so she had to grip the steering wheel hard, as though she was holding onto dear life itself. Her life.

But the day she was driving to her uncle's sixty-fifth birthday, the Mustang behaved peculiarly, as if it had an un-yielding mind of its own, a mind Fiona could not control, manipulate. It made recurring jerky movements—she even stalled it a couple of times which annoyed her. Luckily, there was no one behind her, or in front. In fact, there were hardly any other vehicles on the road. She felt the shaky, clattering machinery of the car reverberate up and down her spine as if a potent, viscid terror had seized her by the waist with its tentacles.

Fiona had anticipated that she'd arrive at her uncle's house in less than three hours. Most of her family members would already be there drinking brandy, martinis, playing board games or eating a roast meal she thought, parked by herself on the side of the road. Her family would be worried about her wouldn't they, if she was late? Wouldn't they contact the police and express their distress? Where could she be? She does know the way doesn't she? She can't be in any kind of trouble? The heating had stopped. Her brother Charlie had asked her the previous day if she wanted to take a ride with him. No, Fiona insisted, she would get there by herself, she'd take a road map, though her brother warned her it was a fairly long drive. There was no one else on the road, and damn it, she'd left her cell phone by mistake in her apartment, and consequently Fiona couldn't call her brother. I'm not going to panic, she was saying, there's no point in panicking, right? Someone will be driving along here soon. I can't be the only one.

Fiona stepped out to examine the car engine. She lifted the hood of the car. A jet of hot, coiling steam hit her face. She assumed the engine had overheated, or the battery had gone flat.

She glanced around. Fiona noticed that she couldn't really see anything. Her doughy face gleamed in the cold and her mouth trembled. She was wearing a knee-length coat and a pair of snake-print boots. Her oak-brown hair was crimped, and she rubbed her hands vigorously together. The sky was like a sheet of burnished aluminium. It was forecasted to snow, a feathery blizzard fermenting somewhere in the distance. Fiona felt a chill in her stomach, as though she'd swallowed a spoonful of grey ice. She turned her head from side to side. There wasn't a vehicle in sight.

Tiny flakes of snow coated her face.

She fumbled in her coat pockets for her keys. It took her a while to hold them. The wind picked up, gently. Fiona got back into the car and slammed the door.

She imagined that she'd be found frozen like a marble slab. Flakes of snow lightly dappled the front and rear windows, and Fiona felt the whiteness throb around her. She thought the coldness would wrap her around in the base of winter—a blanket of sleet or hail curled over her legs, her neck. Fiona tried to remain in a calm state of mind. There was a mini bottle of rum she'd brought with her. She always liked to drink a little when driving. The rum felt warm, soothing, as it slivered down her dry throat.

Fiona tried to switch the engine on again. It failed to start. Once, it made a roaring sound, feebly, and the wheels spun and she gasped but it went dead again straight away. She looked at her watch. Forty minutes had passed. It was after four o'clock but Fiona had planned to be at her uncle's by two-thirty in the afternoon. Her family would be concerned about her whereabouts, especially because she had a habit of being punctual; she was, as her mother had teasingly said at a dinner party, notorious for it. This is not typical of her, she guessed her brother Charlie would remark. She pressed her right foot, harshly, on the gas pedal, then on the clutch, as if the car would mysteriously come to life.

She was thinking, I have to do so something! I can't stay locked in here like a mute! I must do something! But what?

Then, when she looked at the side-view mirror she saw two orbs of yellow light. It couldn't be, could it? Was another vehicle approaching through the midst of all that whiteness? She lowered the window, poked her head out, and heard the distant sound of an engine. Fiona's heart beat faster. She opened the door, leapt out, and scuttled to the middle of the road. Her boots grated against the hard, pebbly surface and Fiona waved her arms in the air.

The truck braked to a thunderous halt, skidding several metres away from her and stopped. A man climbed out and shouted, "What the hell were you thinkin'! Are you crazy! I could have killed you!"

He marched up to her. He was a slim man, with a stubbly face and deep-set grey eyes. He wore a baseball cap, a heavy jacket and corduroy trousers. For an instant, she thought she knew him but he was unfamiliar. When he drew close, she saw that he was the same height as her. There was snow speckled on his brows.

"I'm so sorry sir," she said, quivering. "I didn't know what else to do. My car has broken down, and I've been stuck here all alone. Can you please help me?"

When he saw that she was distressed and shivering with pale lips, his features softened. Fiona was gladdened by the change in his tone, which was more empathetic than belligerent. He suggested that he should take a look at the car to see what was wrong. She was thankful that someone was willing enough to help her and maybe he'd be able to fix the problem, and then she could be on her way again. Of course, she would give him money if he managed to repair the car. Even if he declined the offer, she'd insist he take the payment. It would only be the polite thing to do.

He peered into the engine then said, "Yep, I reckon you've got a dead battery. There ain't nothin' I can do miss. But there's a garage less than fifteen miles from here. I can give you a ride there if you like?"

Fiona wasn't certain if she should hop into a truck with a total stranger she had only known for a couple of minutes. Would it be wise? She definitely did not want to remain in the cold by herself. The man gawped at her, as if to say Well, are you comin' or not? Or would you prefer freezin' to death?

"Thank you," she said finally. "That's very kind of you. But what about my car?"

He banged the hood down. "You don't have to fret about that miss," he said. She thought she saw the falling snow reflected in his eyes. "Not a soul will dare lay a finger on it. It'll be safe here, I promise you."

Fiona clambered into his truck, and sat on the passenger's seat on the right, with her personal belongings in her bag. There were movie magazines scattered on the floor, but he told her she could rest her feet on them. She shuddered. Fiona strapped herself, and held the belt as firmly as she could. Her breasts were squashed, her thigh muscles taut. She pushed the magazines under the seat with the heel of her boots, then pressed her knees together. Her breathing was heavy, then quiet, as if her lungs were stippled with gaping holes.

Her hair was coated with melting snow.

"Off we go," the man said jovially and he steered the truck into a proper position to drive off in. There was saliva glossed on his lower lip. She stared at her Mustang as he drove past. Fiona wondered if she'd made the right decision by leaving it unattended.

"Where you headin' off to?" he said. He'd taken off his baseball cap, and his hair was straw-like, matted. He had a chunky silver ring on his middle finger on the left hand. Fiona didn't object to being asked such a question. She thought he was merely attempting to start a friendly conversation, a way of passing their time together.

"To my uncle's," she said, facing him. "It's his birthday."

"An old man is he?"

"He's sixty-five," she said, her voice a little shaky.

"Nice," he said. He nodded his head and grinned. "Real nice." The skin around his eyes was folded into pleats.

Fiona's heart wasn't beating as hard as it had been: it was steady and determined. She turned her head away from the man. Occasionally, he glanced at her, but she seemed not to notice or pay attention. Fiona didn't think she'd consciously plunged herself in grave danger by travelling with a stranger. After all, he was helping her wasn't he? Instead, it was the whiteness outside that mesmerized her. It had stopped snowing, but the sky was endless and refulgent. Fiona felt the whiteness crawling across her face as she pressed her cheek against the window. She thought she saw trees, emaciated, with winding branches. Aside from that, it was only the whiteness and the sky.

She inhaled audibly. The air was musty inside the truck. It was 4:45 p.m.

"So what's your name, if you don't mind my askin'?" the man said. She wasn't sure if he'd winked at her, or smirked. Was he watching her curiously when she'd been looking out of the window?

"It's Fiona."

He started to cough, gratingly, and said, "I apologise . . . I'm Gary." Fiona noticed then that his voice was guttural, raspy. He laughed and said, "Can't believe I forgot to tell you my own name! A cagey guy huh?"

"I suppose so," she said nervously.

He went on to tell her that he was a deliveryman but did not specify what he delivered. He'd been doing this kind of work for five years, and had met countless number of interesting people. In his spare time, he worked as a domestic repairman—he had taught himself—and could mend anything from a defective radio to a tumble dryer. He enjoyed it and it gave him extra money.

Fiona only listened partly to what he said. She was hoping to get to the garage soon. She gripped the seat belt tighter. "How far is it now to the garage?" she said, interrupting him as he was saying something about where he lived. She looked at him tensely.

"Not far," he said. "Not far at all."

The whiteness gradually faded. It didn't appear as impenetrable as before. She began to see small clusters of new houses and deciduous trees. The snow on the road lay in peaks of mush.

Fiona was hunched back on her seat and she gazed dreamily, unblinking, but suddenly she lurched forward and said, "That's the garage we just passed isn't it?" She knew she'd seen it, it wasn't a mistake, a mirage.

"Oh," he said, "it sure is."

"Well shouldn't you have stopped?" There was an agitation in her voice and she felt a wrinkle of moisture run down her temples, into her ears. He grasped the steering wheel as hard as he could, and his knuckles were sallow, scabrous. He drove faster. The truck swerved, and she saw how his eyes puffed and shrunk back to their ordinary size.

Her heart was beating hard in her chest. Her face was flushed.

"I thought we could go for a drink," he said. "You've been out in the cold for a while, you sure need somethin' hot to drink."

"But—"

"Plus I'm hungry, we could eat somethin'. There's a little diner round the corner here that I know." He glanced at her in a flash. Fiona quavered, and a sudden sense of helplessness jabbed at her. She felt foolish, isolated. She didn't want to cry. That's not the kind of person she was, to cry like a child.

He cleared his throat with a ripping, lacerating sound like he'd swallowed a lump of phlegm.

"We'll go to the garage later," he said sniffing. "We can just grab somethin' to eat first. It won't take forever, and then you'll be on your way." He pressed the brake pedal, lowered the gear, and entered into a side road on the left. She hadn't noticed it before, but he had a tattoo on his neck, below the jawline, where his skin was raw, a squiggly symbol she couldn't decode. He looked at her with raised eyebrows and in a coaxing voice said, "You seem shaken. Honestly, it won't take very long. I'm only tryin' to be neighbourly."

Did he laugh or frown at her? His teeth were tainted and uneven. He smiled, then concentrated on the driving and he accelerated through a sequence of loops and bends.

She could see nothing ahead.

Fiona thought, No! I'll get through this! No one is going to harm me! She was thinking if she'd said something erroneous, something to give the wrong impression. Wasn't he capable of leaning towards her and strangling her, or punching her, knocking her out, or maiming her, doing some real physical damage which would leave her permanently scarred, disfigured? She thought, Did I make a remark that led him to believe that he could take me for a drink? Am I to blame? Is this my fault?

Her scalp felt blistered and she said to herself, I'm fine, I've always been fine, no one has ever harmed me. No one ever will.

The truck came to a jarring, bouncy stop. "This is it," he said. Fiona did not know where she was. She saw no car park. It was as if she'd lost all possible sensation in her body, like she'd been sedated or hypnotised. She knew he'd switched lanes, but she wasn't clear on what she'd seen pass by—a fox? Another vehicle? A Deer? A darting hare? Or had she heard a horn blaring? Fiona was aware of Gary sitting next to her, she could hear his raspy breathing, and she tried to absorb the fact that perhaps, for once, she was not in total control. Bubbles of cold sweat popped out of her skin, under her knees, on her lips.

Gary said, taking the key out of the ignition, "The diner is right over there, can you see it?" He pointed at it with his finger.

Fiona turned her head, swiftly. He was correct—about fifty yards in front, she saw a low-roofed building with the name Comfort Grille blinking in pink neon lights. She squinted. There was no doubt in her mind that it wouldn't be

26

wise of her to run. She thought, As long as I remain assured and composed, he can't do anything. Plus, he's taking me to a public place, he wouldn't be able to do anything anyway. And if he does . . .

"The truck is safe here," he said. "We'll be quick, I promise." He watched her. He was waited for her to make a move; he waited for her to speak. "Shouldn't you take off your seat belt?" he said and he tugged the sleeves of his jacket.

At first, she did not reply. Her eyes were glazed and Fiona unbuckled the belt and she said, because she knew she couldn't remain silent, "Will the garage still be open? I need to be on my way soon." She stammered, and her voice was somewhat childish. He grinned at her.

"There ain't no need to worry," he said. "Are you ready?"

"Yes, yes I am," she said.

Fiona leaned her head down under the seat to pick her bag up. She hadn't noticed it before, but there was a hammer, no bigger than a screwdriver, beneath the passenger seat. I'd be able to strike him with that! It would easily crack his skull. He was outside, smoking a cigarette, his back facing the truck. She brushed her hair back with a hand, then went out as well.

Like a glove, she slipped the hammer discreetly into her bag.

The diner smelled brackish to her, and there was a whiff of roasting ham. It was brightly lit and smoky. There was jangly, rock music playing from the jukebox. Gary was stood in front of her, and she peered over his shoulder to see the mini TV screen flashing on the counter—a woman in pearl earrings reading the news, whilst the trees behind her swayed viciously, and the wind whipped her hair. A storm developing somewhere.

He gestured with his hand for her to follow him to the corner of the diner.

It wasn't a big diner. The décor was mustard coloured—the seats, the cushions—and the wallpaper was plain, the floor mantled in varnished wooden boards, and a bunch of fake plastic flowers in each vase on the tables. There were a group of men seated together on one of the tables, eating fried food and flirting with the waitresses, making bawdy remarks. There were three waitresses, and one of them was elderly and working behind the counter. She was chubby with wiry hair. Her curved face was embellished with heavy make-up, though Fiona could see that in her youth she must have been pretty and slim. She imagined her to be once like those sultry, pouty-mouthed women she'd seen in glamour magazines advertising toothpaste with wide smiles. The two younger waitresses had dyed hair, blonde, and their roots were dark.

After a moment the elderly waitress came over and said, "Do you want a table?" He replied, Yes, he did want one, and would like to sit in the corner next to the window. "You've been here before haven't you?" she asked him, and he said he had, a couple of months ago. "I thought I recognised your face," she said, "I don't really forget people's faces." Her lashes were curled like claws and veneered in blue-black mascara.

Fiona sat opposite him. She took her coat off, letting it drop over the seat, and she placed her bag on the floor. There was a picture of a horse on the wall, which she thought was incompatible with the style of the diner. She felt light-headed. She was suspicious of the other men whispering about her.

Walking to the diner, she thought about pulling the hammer out. She knew she had the chance to strike it brutally against his head and poke it through his brain. Fiona could have done it easily, she knew that, and then she'd have driven away in his truck. But something prevented her from doing so. But what was it? Was it Cowardice? Timidity? A devouring weakness? For a minute Fiona didn't know where to look, and her eyes were like washed glass.

They both leafed through the menu. She wondered if Gary was glimpsed up at her with his face twisted in a contemptuous smile. He asked her what she was going to have. She reread the menu rapidly because she hadn't really read it initially and her fingers were moist as she skimmed through the pages. Fiona wondered what her family members were doing—if they were puzzled or anxious about her whereabouts; and her car—would it be in the exact place she'd left it? Had it been broken into and vandalised? One of the younger waitresses took their order, and her manner was both obliging and surly as if in a bad temper, she were forced to be civil to her customers. Her nails were long and painted in clear varnish. Fiona ordered a hot chocolate. "Is that it?" he said, and she told him, not completely at ease, "Yes, I'm not very hungry." In truth, she could have eaten a full bowl of parsnip soup and a plate of char-grilled steak with sautéed vegetables, but she shook her head and said, "I'll be OK with the hot chocolate, honestly I'll be OK." She did not wish to eat food in his company. That would be too intimate as if she was skinless in his presence. He ordered a glass of ginger beer and a hamburger.

The men on the other table burst into a fit of raucous laughter. She asked the waitress if there was a phone she could use. "There is one," the waitress said, "but it's out of order."

"Tryin' to call someone?" he said.

"Yes, a family member. They'll want to know where I am."

He lit a cigarette and smoked it audibly. He stared at her. There were wrinkles ridged along his forehead. She guessed he was in his mid-thirties to early-forties.

A ripple of smoke billowed out of his nostrils.

"You thought I was gonna hurt you?" he said. "Didn't you?"

Fiona looked up at him fully then. The wrinkles on his forehead were arched. She felt a frantic palpitation, like a feral bird flapping witlessly inside her, a stab in her groin. Her face seemed to close in. There was a strained silence— the cacophony of a jangly song playing on the jukebox, the harshness of laughter in the background.

The waitress brought their order over and placed it on the table.

"No," she said, not quite eyeing him properly. "W-what gave you that impression?" She laughed nervously.

"I could tell," he said and he crushed the cigarette in the ashtray. She saw a crackle of fiery amber light burn in the ashtray, then fade away. "You weren't talkin' much whilst I was drivin'. I just knew."

"No seriously . . . I'm . . . I'm, I apologise if I . . . if I gave you . . ." She couldn't finish her sentence.

"It doesn't matter Fiona," he said. There was a softness in his voice she hadn't detected before. "You don't need to explain anythin'. I understand."

There was a tingling in her ears, muddled with the music from the jukebox. Fiona was about to open her mouth when he said whimsically, "Truly, it don't bother me. My wife will probably laugh when I tell her this!"

"You have a wife?"

"Yep," he said, "and three kids."

Fiona did not know what else to say. She sat silently and listened to him as he spoke in a relaxed voice. There was an air of light-heartedness about him. He showed her a slightly creased picture of his family together with him, which he pulled out of his wallet. His wife had short hair and wore a turquoise blouse. Fiona wondered what she sounded like when she spoke. "That's my boy Sam," he said, pointing at

30

the photograph, "he's a real neat kid, and that's baby Leah, and that's my other girl Toni. I sure do miss 'em when I'm on the road."

"They all seem nice," she said.

"They sure are."

She sighed.

"You ain't touched your drink yet," he said. She hadn't noticed the waitress put it on her side of the table, nor did she notice him eat. His plate and glass were both empty. The hot chocolate was dark, milky, and she felt the tightness in her leg muscles diminish.

"It's doesn't matter," she said, "I didn't want it anyway."

"Well, we should head off to the garage," he said. "Don't want you to be late for your uncle's party." He stood up. "Christ!" he said, his mouth gaping. "It's snowin' again."

She saw bristles of snow drifting with the wind, and the sky twinkled, mile after mile.

Severing through the same curves and bends, he drove hurriedly and in silence to the garage, which turned out to be not so far from the Comfort Grille as she'd thought. At the garage reception he made the arrangements, and clarified the problem with her car while she waited in the truck.

Fiona felt guilty because he didn't allow her to pay at the diner, but he was adamant that he pay. "It's not everyday I get the chance to take someone out!" She looked troubled then, like someone who wasn't sure where they were, or what they were doing.

Eager to make conversation, Fiona 'thank you' to him more than once, and asked him rather wistfully if she could pay him back—she realised it wasn't much, but it was a matter of principle. "Let me tell you again," he said, half-angrily, "if I wanted you to pay, I would have asked you, hell I might have ran away! It ain't no big crime buyin' someone a drink, is it?"

She shrugged without saying anything further.

A mechanic followed behind them as they drove back to where her Mustang was. The snow was falling like a huge, flailing scarf, but her eyes weren't tired. She instantly saw where her car was, left in the place she'd broken down, and she was relieved that it hadn't been ravaged.

Fiona sat with him patiently in the truck whilst the mechanic, a man with burly shoulders fixed the car. "Hope I didn't hold you up a while," Gary said. "I 'spose you have reason to be mad."

"I'm not mad," she said, meeting his eyes.

"Looks like your car is done." He rubbed his hands together.

The mechanic added up the bill, including tax. It totalled to more than she'd expected, but she was given ten working days to pay it within. Fiona folded the receipt and tucked it into her coat pocket. She got back into the Mustang. It was cold, and the steering wheel felt stiff. Gary shouted from his truck, "Have a safe journey!"

She blinked at him. The snow whirled. She liked him, suddenly. "I will," she said.

Fiona exhaled and reclined back on to a familiar seat. She watched him drive away, the rear lights of the truck glowing red, then gone. It was 7:40 p.m. She unfolded the roadmap on her lap. She didn't know what explanation she'd give her family when they'd ask her repetitively, What kept you? Were you in any kind of danger? Are you hurt anywhere? Did the police stop you? You are telling us the truth aren't you? You're not keeping anything from us? Fiona unzipped her bag. Annoyed and bemused, she couldn't comprehend why she'd stolen his hammer. She clearly couldn't return it to him.

She thought about flinging it out of the window, but instead, she patted it and kept it in her bag.

Fiona wondered if the blizzard had started, if it stirred behind her. She saw her face in the interior mirror, salmon-pink, and her fringe was tousled. She started the Mustang and switched the wipers on. The car joggled to begin with then ran smoothly. Fiona drove off into the snow.

SARAH WYNN

The Distinguished Professor of Tarot Stones

One by one he separates them
into piles, each falling lightly
onto the desk, the sound sharp
and then fading to echo, each
stone hitting the wood different,
the quartz, sodalite, azure,
desert rose, carnelian.

Asked why he says
so I can tell who they are,
so I can hear them breathing.

He explains the difference between
the categories and how even things
that aren't living have souls.

Then, he returns to the stones
out of respect and keeps sorting,
one by one, his thin fingers moving easily
in the spaces between the agate
and the malachite.

J. M. SHIVELELY

Do You Ever Get Lonely?

Ted Chiles

Love Under an Invisible Hand

The rising sun shone through the gaps of wooden blinds warming the headboard. Mara woke first because it was her house, and it was the last day. The list of morning chores that followed her into bed still weighed on her as she searched Mathew's face for something different, some heterogeneous trait in the shape of his nose or the grain of his beard. She saw nothing to set him apart from the men before him or the man she'd contract with tonight.

Her finger traveled the ridge of his ear to the lobe and then moved to his chest, gathered his hairs and twirled them together as if to make yarn. His eyes opened and he lifted his head off the pillow pushing his elbows into the mattress her hand rising with his chest until he paused looking at her. When she saw his recognition, she straddled him, knowing she would never see him again.

They shared a breakfast of coffee, croissants, butter and blackberry jam—her usual Friday fare. Mara wanted the last few minutes of the contract to be infused with a per-manency, yet she knew this scene was being played out by thousands of Maras and Mathews in the same kitchens in the same houses across the town. This Friday ended, as all before had without her being set apart from the others.

"Are you going tonight?" he asked.

"Yes. You?"

"I'm going to buy. Will you sell?"

"I haven't decided."

Mathew finished his coffee and glanced at the clock above the sink and like every man on every Friday, he stood, smiled and said, "It's time." They both gathered satchels and umbrellas, his and hers identical in shape, size and color, and walked to the door. On the step, Mara turned to Mathew and kissed him. He returned the kiss, as they all did before him, nodded and said, "Goodbye," walking south toward the subway.

Mara stayed on the steps. Waiting. Hoping that some tactile memory or scent or awareness she had conveyed would cause him to slow his step. Then puzzled, he would turn to look for her because in their parting, he would finally know that she was different. Not in the texture of hair or the timber of voice, because all Maras were indistinguishable as were all Mathews, but in her nature. That would set her apart. She knew she was unique. And the Mathew who could discern her uniqueness would also be distinct. But this Friday, as last Friday and all those she remembered, he just kept walking and when he turned the corner, Mara went north.

At 5:30 p.m. the doors to the office buildings opened, and the workers flowed onto the street. Mara was in the second wave and before her the sidewalk was awash with the blue dresses and grey suits of those heading towards the market. She looked back and saw among the ineligible—the old and marked—five or six younger workers going home. Their youth a glaring counterpoint. Mara wondered what the sadness or complacency that turned them against the current? In front of her, most diverted themselves into the taverns that lined the street. Deciding against her customary glass of wine, Mara approached the small park at the entrance to the market named after a distinguished Auctioneer.

She stopped at the coffee cart.

"Yes miss," asked the coffee vendor. He was too old for the market and had lost most of his hair but used what remained to break the uniformity of his scalp.

"One please," Mara said.

As he handed her the cup, she inadvertently stroked his finger in the exchange. The muscles surrounding his mouth relaxed and his jaw dropped, not theatrically but delicately and Mara felt that he was remembering that odd mixture of arousal and apprehension when he had approached the market. She watched as he regained focus and sensed a resentment forming in him of her and all in her circumstances, that none earned but were endowed by their youth.

She didn't appease him with an excessive tip.

Sipping her coffee, she inspected each passing male. This week I will buy and move into his house, she thought and then pulled the two pieces of fabric from her satchel. Both a square foot of smooth silk hemmed with a cross-stitch: one red and one white, a tender and an assent. She fingered the assent still smooth and shiny. The red tender had begun to fade and a thread dangled from the corner. Mara held it to her teeth and bit the thread, then placed the tender in her pocket and followed with the assent. He will have all the same things; his bed is as firm, the linens as soft. She stood as if to mark the decision and tossed the cold remnants of her coffee into the green wire barrel noting she could have made better.

Mara walked through the gate of the marketplace. Its immensity and the uniformity of the structure, a perfect circle that could hold thousands, seemed unnatural as if a gift left one night by some other race or species. She turned right and entered the tender area designated by a red circle. She strolled the perimeter, occasionally trailing her finger along the smooth wall as she weighed the composition of the crowd, and entered the white border of the assent area.

At the bell the buyers moved to the right, brandishing their assents. Mara pulled hers from her pocket and started to follow but after three steps turned and joined the sellers to the left exchanging the red for the white cloth. The Auctioneer climbed the steps to the platform, and the market became silent as if struck dumb by some god.

Mara considered the Auctioneer as he gauged the crowd. He's old, but he doesn't hide his age. He uses it as a claim.

"The Terms of Trade are 250 units," he announced.

Mara quickly converted the terms to wages and then to the duties of the seller: washing, cleaning, feeding and loving of the buyer. It was 1⅔ day's wage, not as low as she feared. She knew that the first price rarely cleared the market and expected that unmatched buyers would drive the price higher.

"Let those willing to trade on these terms come forward and offer a contract," the Auctioneer said.

Mara moved forward, but many stood their ground, forcing her to weave around them. She entered the trading area formed by the intersection of the white and red circles. The buyers and seller randomly sorted themselves, displaying the red or white handkerchiefs. Mara moved among them, glancing at several but never stopping until she was the last to offer a contract. A man approached, she lifted her tender and he raised his assent in acceptance. They turned towards the Auctioneer and saw, as he did, that many buyers stood in the intersection with assents but without contacts.

"The market has not cleared. The Terms are rescinded. Reform," the Auctioneer said.

Mara returned to the seller's side.

"The Terms of Trade are 268 units."

Again the buyers and sellers mixed, but this time the excess was in those who offer to sell. The group separated and reformed twice until at 259 each buyer had a seller.

"The market has cleared and these contracts shall bind until the morning of Friday hence," the Auctioneer said.

Mara looked up at Mathew. His hair, his ears and the shape of his mouth were the same. And when she kissed him, so was his taste.

The rising sun shone through the gaps of the wooden blinds and heated the headboard. Mara awoke first because it was her house and it was the last day and because her morning chores beckoned. She studied this Mathew's face for something different, some eccentricity in the lines around his eye or the sound of his breathe, but nothing set him apart from the men before him or those to come.

Her finger traveled the ridge of his ear to his lobe and then moved to his chest, brushing his nipple, and then descended to arouse him. He awoke rushing into consciousness, disoriented and alarmed, but then he saw Mara and smiled and let his body fall back into the mattress. She rose and settled onto him.

They shared a breakfast of croissants, butter, blackberry jam and coffee. She wanted this time, the final few moments to be infused with a permanency, but each Friday ended without her being set apart from all the others. And she knew this scene was being played out by thousands of Maras and Mathews across the town.

"Are you going tonight?" he asked.

"Yes," she said

"Will you sell?"

"Probably."

Mathew finished his coffee and glanced at the clock above the sink, he stood and smiled and said, "It's time." They both gathered their satchels and umbrellas and walked to the door. On the step, Mara turned to Mathew and kissed him.

He opened his mouth wider and captured her lower lip with his teeth and bit softly. Mara felt the pressure and before she could protest warmth filled her chest and spread like a glass of wine tipped over by a drunken man. And like that man she watched perplexed as it spread across the whiteness of the tablecloth until the blush had stained her.

Mathew released her lip and said, "Goodbye," and began to walk south toward the subway. Mara called out to him, "Mathew." He stopped and turned, and she still couldn't discern any singular feature to identify him from all the others.

"I will carry a rose," Mara said.

"Why?"

"So you can find me," she said and headed north.

Mathew sat alone on a single seat in the subway car. Next to him were three males who each carried the same satchel and umbrella and were dressed as he was in a dark grey suit, white shirt and red tie. Opposite two females wore dark blue dresses. The same dress he watched walk away from him ten minutes ago. Why would she want to repeat our contract? We are all the same like the umbrellas we carry. Each umbrella made by some small firm, one of hundreds. Could you pick one out from another? No, they are identical, interchangeable. As am I. And so is she. No different from the two who sit across from me. Why would she want me to seek her out?

Mathew gazed at the young women. He enjoyed the shape of their necks and the way their hair teased their collars. Why would I prefer one to the other? No difference could be found by measurement or discerned by an impartial panel of judges.

The answer came to him as he examined the women in their blue dresses. For he began to imagine that the woman on the right might have a variation in her face. Is her left eye lower? He found the thought of a deviation both disconcerted and excited him, and then he knew. Mara believes I'm different.

What could have brought this on? Caused her to set me apart. Was it some random act? Mathew felt his muscles give and his posture curve like some soft pliable mass exploring the contours of a new surface.

It doesn't matter.

She believes I'm different and has acted upon it, and that action made it true. Makes it the truth. I am different. Better. And she will offer more.

Mara sat drinking wine alone. She surveyed the tavern, then dropped her hand to the satchel, opened the clasp and looked down. The rose lay on top of the red cloth. She touched the stem as if to ensure its existence and slowly drew her finger to a thorn and pressed until the thorn pierced her finger. A drop of blood slowly bloomed. Mara let the blood run onto the tender, hoping that it would renew its shine. But it was darker and did not blend.

She took her finger in her mouth and sucked the wound and signaled the barkeeper. He brought a new glass and took the old. She held it up to the light and viewed the tavern through its red filter and then sipped the wine, rolling it on her tongue, separating the sensations. Then the door opened and the others poured in.

Twenty minutes later Mara entered the market. Turned to the sellers' side and walked to the rear.

Mathew walked the perimeter, looking for the flower and he brushed by Mara but didn't recognize her. When the bell rang, he walked through the buyer's circle and stood on the front edge of the white line clutching his assent.

The bell rang and Mara extracted the rose from her satchel and moved to the front the sellers. The Auctioneer declared the terms of trade, and Mara walked forward, clutching her rose tightly to her chest with her left hand and extending her

44

tender in her right. A man approached, almost in a trot, yet he didn't raise his assent. Instead, he stood in front of her. Hesitating. After a moment, he leaned down and whispered into her ear, "Will you offer a premium?"

Mara asked, "The amount?"

"Ten percent."

Mara stiffened as he stepped back and lifted his assent. She lifted her tender, and they turned towards the Auctioneer.

"The market has not cleared. The Terms are rescinded. Reform"

Mara watched Mathew walk back, marked his location and returned to the seller's side. The woman next to her frowned as she saw the flower.

At the announcement of the new Terms, Mara moved towards Mathew who walked towards her, but two women moved in front of her. Then a man appeared offering his assent. Mara tilted her head and waited. He didn't lean forward. He didn't request a premium. Instead, he stood gazing at her rose with his assent held in front of him. Mara lowered her head. He left but someone else approached.

"Do you offer a premium?"

Mara nodded.

The market cleared, and Mara leaned in, kissed him and pulled back, moved to him. He captured her lower lip lightly in his teeth. Mara again felt the warmth in her chest when a voice behind her said, "The Auctioneer would like to speak with both of you."

The richness of the Auctioneer's office lay in the antiquity of the furnishings. Old heavy wood, though plain in design, from a time when variation in production occurred, and firms offered unique products. Inherited by all who hold the post, this temporary throne could only be retained by skill.

Mara wondered why he interviewed Mathew first.

The Auctioneer sat quietly writing. Mara studied his hands. The fingers were long and thin without the spots or blemishes often found on one of his age. He wore a ring on the second finger of his right hand with the seal of his office, the intersection of two perfectly symmetric circles with each circle offering the other an equal share.

"Why did you bring the flower to the market?" the Auctioneer asked.

Mara looked up and after a moment said, "Is there some reason that I shouldn't have?"

"That depends on the answer."

Mara said nothing. The Auctioneer waited. Mara crossed her ankles tilting her left foot so that it balanced on the edge of the sole of her shoe.

"Did you expect a spot of red in a sea of blue and grey to go unnoticed. The flower was not visible until the Terms were offered. Why was that?" he asked.

"You're mistaken. I didn't conceal the flower. I carried it in my satchel," she said.

The Auctioneer paused, made a note on the paper in front of him. Mara moved her feet and crossed them with the right foot now underneath.

"I saw the other participants observe you. Many paused and in the second round one approached. You did not accept his offer. Can you tell me why?"

"It's a free market."

"Yes it is, but why enter the intersection if you're not planning to sell?"

"I was on the margin. Indifferent."

"I simply wish to know why you refused the first offer but not the one from the man in the anteroom?"

"As I said, I was on the margin."

The auctioneer nodded and made another note on the paper in front of him.

"You are not different. Neither is he. You know that all are uniform and an adornment is a waste. It will have no impact. Any gain you expect by this differentiation will be exposed during the contract."

Mara wanted to hurl something, anything at him. She uncrossed her feet and pressed back into the chair.

The Auctioneer smiled and then said, "The flower interfered. It was a distraction and hindered the contracting process. It will not be allowed. You will not bring a flower next Friday or attempt to differentiate yourself in any manner. If you do, you will be ejected, banned and branded. Do you understand?"

"Yes."

"If you alter yourself in any visible manner even if by accident, you will be banned and branded. Am I clear?"

Mara nodded.

"A verbal answer is required," he said.

"Yes. I understand."

"You may go," he said.

Mara stood and tried to read what he had written on the paper but couldn't. She turned and walked towards the door, but as her hand grasped the doorknob, the Auctioneer said, "One last thing."

She turned to face him.

"If you were different, he wouldn't need a flower to find you. Would he?"

Mara sat cross-legged on her bed studying the contours of Mathew's face. His soft snores mixed with her breathing. He looked younger in the lamplight. She brushed his hair with her fingertips. She has done this each night for last six and still there was no hint of his singularity. No difference marks him from all the others of his age. Men. They are identical as is each blade of grass. As is each snowflake.

But he is different. His touch. His taste. The feel of him is unique. And that I can recognize. His touch makes me unique. I must find him again.

But how?

"I won't go against the Auctioneer. I won't risk being branded," he told her again today.

She turned off the lamp and stretched out next to him, molding herself to him. Pressing her pelvis to his buttock and her breasts to his shoulder blades. A small bruise had formed on the top of her right hip and the faint outline of a bite mark decorated her shoulder. His movement had urgency, and with each passing night the coupling grew rougher. She had never felt so taken and at the same time so filled. Completed. Different. I cannot lose this man and return to the tedium of the market. The boredom would ruin me. She moved against him as if displacing the air between them. He slid away, but she pursued him across the bed until the edge contained him. She buried her nose in his hair and inhaled the scent. Trying to quiet her mind.

The next afternoon Mara unpacked the groceries: two bottles of red wine instead of one, a larger cut of beef and extra mushrooms joined the greens and potatoes. The single rose lay on the table. She checked the bill, fifteen percent higher than the Terms. She wondered if he would notice.

She turned on the oven and began to wash the greens.

Mathew walked in, kissed her and opened a bottle of wine. Poured two glasses and sat watching her. She lifted the greens from the water and laid them on a white cloth towel. Took a potato and scrubbed it. The muscles of her neck tensed and he imagined himself pressing into her and watching the back of her neck tighten with the effort of it.

She dried the potato and reached for the second.

48

He studied the rose on the table and wondered if there was some way to find each other safely at the market. This arrangement had its benefits.

"You're taking that are you?" he asked.

"I won't need it," she said.

Mara took a small knife and pierced the skins of the potatoes, rubbed them with oil and salt. She opened the oven door and the heat briefly lifted the ends of her hair as she bent down to put in the potatoes. Taking a sip of her wine, she picked up a damp cloth to clean the mushrooms.

He reached for the wine, filled his glass and tilted the bottle toward her.

"I'm fine," she said.

Mathew inclined in the chair and drank as she cut the mushrooms.

"I like them sliced thicker," he said.

She stopped with the knife posed above the cutting board, but then cut another mushroom and held it up for his inspection.

"Perfect," he said.

After dinner Mara washed the dishes, and Mathew sat on the coach drinking. When she finished, she sat next him. He picked up the wine and looked at her with his eyebrows raised.

"No. You finish it," she said.

He emptied the bottle and said, "It has been a good week."

"Would you contract with me again?" she asked.

"Yes, but what are the chances?"

"But if we could?"

"I won't risk being branded."

Mara took the glass from his hand and sipped some of his wine. Then she placed it on the end table and grasped his hands. He looked down. His nails were perfect. Equal in shade and arc. Every nail a perfect balance of white and pink. Hers were uneven. Some normal, filed in smooth arcs of equal length and painted red, but the nail on the first finger of her right hand was deformed. Ragged and chipped. The little finger's nail had been picked at until it tore. They lacked uniformity. They were ugly.

Mathew looked up and saw in her a need for him. She aches for me, and it has turned her in some way, he thought.

"I offer you a contract. For the coming week, and the following week, and every week after that," Mara said.

Mathew pulled his hands from her grasp and laughed, reclaiming the glass.

"That's absurd. How would we set the terms?" he asked.

"I offer the same as this week."

"But our terms derive from the market. Anyway, it's illegal."

"I know you've enjoyed me."

"I did, but a 10% premium isn't worth the risk."

Mara pressed her arms to her sides.

"How much do you need?"

And he told her. For a minute she simply sat there with her hands in her lap. Then she stood, took his hand and led him up the stairs to her bed. Focusing on the back of her neck, slender and taunt, he followed her.

If she cried, he couldn't tell.

Mara woke first, but it wasn't due to the rising sun that shone through the gaps of the wooden blinds or her list of chores. Mara woke first because Mathew had shifted, and when his arm moved onto her shoulder, her body arose in protest of what it had suffered. She climbed from the bed and walked to the shower, turning the water as hot as she could tolerate.

They shared a breakfast of coffee, croissants, butter and blackberry jam. Mathew finished his coffee and glanced at the clock above the sink. He stood, smiled and said, "It's time." They both gathered their satchels and umbrellas and walked to the door. On the step, Mara turned to Mathew and kissed him.

He opened his mouth wider and captured her lower lip with his teeth, bit softly and again the warmth spread. He increased the pressure, and Mara tried to pull away but then surrendered to it. He released her lip and pulled back.

"What time will you come tonight?" she asked.

"About eight," he said. "The market will have ended, and it will be dark. None will know that we did not join the others."

"I need to go to the grocery. I'll be home by 7:30," she said.

He gave a short nod and walked south.

Mara watched him until he turned the corner. It took her longer than usual to reach her subway station. She smiled at all who passed.

Mara sat at the table. The first bottle of wine was gone, and she had uncorked another to let it breathe. She stood and walked to the refrigerator, opened the door. The chicken sat on a metal platter surrounded by roasted carrots, turnips and onions. A glass bowl held the salad. She reached for a leaf of lettuce and took a bite. The green was crisp and bitter, unpleasant by itself but added balance to the sweetness of the peppers and tomatoes.

Condensation began to form on the glass bowl.

Mara closed the door, took her glass, walked past the stairs and lay on the couch. It was closer to the door.

Mara approached the small park at the entrance to the market. She stopped at the cart and ordered a cup of coffee.

The old vendor handed her the cup and said, "A lovely evening for it."

Mara didn't answer at first but then looked around the park and said, "Yes. It is." She handed him the coins for the coffee and sat on a bench near the entrance to the Market.

When Mara saw the first male approach, she put her cup on bench, reached into her satchel and pulled a rose, placing it across her lap. She sat there quietly. She did not speak. She waited. At first groups of two or three passed and then more came until a steady flow of men and woman walked by her. She held the glance of all who looked her way. But no one stopped. No one spoke to her.

When all had entered the Market, Mara returned the flower to her satchel, finished her coffee, and stood. An official of the market positioned by the entrance watched her. She made no gesture toward him, just turned to go home.

Three Fridays later a man sat next to her on the bench. Is he the one? Mara moved her coffee closer and declined her head in greeting. The man returned the gesture and drank some of his coffee. The movement to the market had just begun. Neither spoke. They sat next to each other and watched the traffic.

"Why do you sit here with that rose?" he asked.

Mara knew then that it was not the man she sought. She glanced at the official by the gate that was watching her. She waited until a large group of females blocked his view and without turning her head, said, "No reason. I like flowers."

"Will you buy or sell tonight?"

"The market no longer interests me."

The man said nothing. He stood, and as he did his coat knocked her coffee off the bench. They both reached for the cup, and their arms crossed. Mara jerked back. The man started to say something but instead went to the cart and bought another cup.

"It was my fault," he said and offered her the coffee.

Mara didn't look up, only shook her head. He put the coffee on the bench and walked towards the entrance. Mara observed the official stop him, and they spoke for a minute. The man entered the market. The official followed. Mara brought the coffee to her lips and sipped before returning her attention to the road. The official returned and approached her.

"The Auctioneer wishes to speak with you. You are to accompany me to his office. He will join you after the market has cleared."

"I have no desire to speak with him," she said and put the rose in the satchel.

"You must."

"Give him my regards," she said.

The Auctioneer sat at her bench with a cup of coffee occupying the other space. At Mara's approach he lifted the coffee and handed her the cup.

"Thank you," she said.

"It isn't from me. It's from a young man who was waiting for you. I promised to deliver it," he said. They sat silently for a while watching the men and women going to the market. Many of who surveyed them with interest.

"He won't come to you," the Auctioneer said.

"I don't know what you're talking about," Mara said.

"The man you signaled that day in the market. The one I interviewed. He won't come to you." He inspected her and then said, "You're not worth the risk. You can sit her for the rest of your time with your flower, and he won't come."

Mara's breath lost its rhythm. She concentrated her gaze on the lowest leaf of the tree by the entrance.

"Did you think that you were the first? That no one else has ever felt drawn."

"It was unique to me." Mara said and raised her head towards the Auctioneer. "I can't go back."

"You might contract with him again."

"I'm not a fool. The probability is zero."

"Then you could find another. If he was different, why do you think he is the only one? Perhaps you are different. Anyone of them would feel different. With you any contract is unique."

Mara smiled at the words. She wanted to believe the Auctioneer, but it had only been with the one man.

"If I'm wrong, it is only a week."

"I couldn't fulfill the contract if you're wrong," she said, and these words were formed without thought or calculation. They came like the horrible declarations of a child. Killing the civility of lies in a room.

"You don't mean that."

"I do."

"If you fail to honor a contract, I will seize your assets," he said. "Will you recant?"

"No."

"Then you're ruined," he said.

They sat quietly until the Auctioneer stood and said, "I should have voided your contract that day. It might have spared you. I am truly sorry."

Mara watched as he entered the market. He stopped and spoke to the guard. She watched all that passed her. When the last person entered and the official at the gate turned his back to watch the proceeding, then she broke. She cried for what might have been and what she had given. No one approached her. When she looked up, the roadway was empty. The park deserted except for the old vendor. She sipped cold black coffee and laughed softly at the perfect cliché of its bitterness. The wind dried her cheeks. She took her tender and assent from the satchel, crushed them into a ball and pushed them into the remnants of her coffee which she tossed at the trash can. The cup missed and settled onto the pavement. The red and white cloths stained by the coffee unfurled.

Two guards exited the marketplace and approached her.

Mara stood, reached into the satchel and dropped the rose on the bench.

LANDIS DUFFETT

Our Digital Future: Nostalgia, Broadcast Television, and the Televisual Sublime

By order of the Federal Communications Commission, on June 12, 2009, all analog transmissions of television in the United States ceased. While network affiliates continue to broadcast their programming free of charge, the future of broadcast television will be digital. Those who own analog TV sets will have to acquire a digital-converter box in order to receive a signal. Of course, analog broadcast television has been an inert technology for almost three decades now anyway. Already in the 1980s, awestruck by Japan's development of high definition television, media analysts were arguing that television as an analog broadcast medium was all but dead. Thus, the FCC's action was not so much an execution as it was euthanasia, pulling the plug on a terminally ill patient with no hope of recovery. The superiority of digital to analog technology in general has become a self-fulfilling truth that only fools, we are told, would contest.

It is not efficiency nor even content that we lost on June 12, but rather, I want to urge, something less tangible, an imaginative capacity, a relationship to a fantasy space that, like the analog signal itself, is neither fully present nor fully absent, neither fully here in the local nor fully in another world beyond the here and now, never, that is, just one or the other, on or off, one or zero. Ultimately, as I hope to show by way of a long detour through my childhood experiences of television in the 1970s, what our televisual future will lack is a unique variety of the feeling of the sublime, what I call the televisual sublime.

Nostalgia is a mournful, narcissistic and, thus, hopelessly impractical emotion. Yet, today it tends to take as its object telecommunication devices (LP players, old TV sets, dial phones) which, while they were still in use, we regarded as nothing more than practical tools for transferring information. It is as if only from a distance in time, only after a piece of technology has been superseded by a more efficient one, do we reflect on that earlier device and convince ourselves, rightly or wrongly, that what we had taken for granted at the time as a simple means to an end had actually been much more than that. As we look back and laugh smugly across the decades at the multi-party telephone line or the messy and tiring ritual of the Polaroid camera, we finally see that this or that media device had been primarily a cultural or social or even aesthetic artifact and only secondarily a technology. We see now that the technology had carried along with it the whole time an unconscious, a bulky, unwieldy and wildly inefficient body that was necessary at the time not so much for the accomplishment of the task, but as support for the part of the device that did directly accomplish the task. As long as we used the technology, though, we directed our gaze away from this unsightly and excessive shell. Indeed, our very embracing of the technology at the time depended upon our ignoring this excess, unable to distinguish it from that single function the technology accomplished.

What we failed to realize then but which we now not only acknowledge but celebrate is that this excessive body, this "unconscious" of the device (the huge irradiated vacuum tubes in old TV sets and radios, for example), provided a fantasy space in which, had we only looked closer, we could have seen reflected our mundane reality but in a less utilitarian and more playful form. Now that we see this space for what it could have been for us at that time, though, it is too late to take full advantage of it. The devices, no longer socially functional and thus no longer a part of our social reality, can no longer offer any resistance to that reality. Rather, caught in our nostalgic gaze, they only reflect back to us our own narcissistic and mournful but still not fully acknowledged desire for a future radically different from the present. And as for recognizing this excess, this unconscious of technology, in the telecommunications devices of today, we simply don't ever seem able to discern it clearly until it is too late.

I attended elementary school in the 1970s, still the golden age of analog broadcast television as well as of another analog medium, the 16mm classroom film. On any given morning, as we sat in our desks chatting, recovering our breath from morning recess, the teacher might proudly announce, "Now we're going to watch a film about x," with x, the topic of the film, emerging out of nowhere with a sudden and exciting randomness. Regardless of the topic, the announcement was always greeted with applause and a palpable but never realized threat of spontaneous carnival or even mutiny. It was as if, through our unusually prolonged applause, we conveyed to the teacher that, while we knew the film was going to be educational and very likely boring, nevertheless we were embracing it—not the film itself but the event—as if it were an unexpected reward or, if not that, then at least an excuse to celebrate something out of the ordinary. I remember watching a film on Greenland in the first grade in 1975. I cannot remember its thrust or theme or any of its linguistic content. I remember only the images of partially melted snow in the summer and vaguely European-looking children standing on a hill, dressed in heavy winter coats, the wind blowing across their ruddy cheeks as they looked out over the vast and desolate arctic plain. Before that film, Greenland did not exist for me. After that film I was obsessed with it, not as a real geographic location, not even as a source of images, but as a fantasy space.

At home I would gaze transfixed for hours at the two pictures that accompanied the article on Greenland in our two-decade old World Book encyclopedia. There it was again, this strange geography of the mind that looked like Missouri, my home, in early March, when the sun illuminates the dirty splotches of snow hovering in the middle of a sea of mud and grass. And there *they* were again, the inhabitants. Who *were* they? *Where* were they? Greenland became a site in my mind for the blending of the exotic and the familiar. My inability to fully grasp this space conceptually only increased my fascination. I continued to cast my gaze far beyond the shiny silver grain elevators visible through the classroom window. Out there somewhere was Greenland, that paradoxical place of endless Christmas vacation, summer in the middle of winter.

Given the increasing fascination that Greenland held for me, it was inevitable that as a fantasy space it would finally merge in my mind with that other great fantasy space of my childhood: television. As a child growing up in the '70s I had my favorite TV shows, just like children of any generation. More than with the content of television, though, I was fascinated with the medium: television in and of itself. It wasn't a fascination with the technological details—of which I still remain largely ignorant (I wasn't a budding engineer who wanted to take things apart and put them together again). What fascinated me was the same thing that fascinated me about Greenland: the intrusive yet beautiful oddness, the uncanny combination of the familiar and the strange.

More than anything I was fascinated with UHF. Unlike the VHF knob that clicked loudly as it flipped discretely from one number to the next, the UHF dial in the 1970s was more like a tuning knob on a radio. I used to sit cross-legged in front of our ridiculously capacious Zenith TV and turn the UHF dial with conscientious precision. Given that TV transmissions traveled through the air, I thought, why couldn't

I—if the weather conditions were right—receive a TV signal from another state or even another country? I knew that if I did ever tune in such a distant signal it would be fuzzy at best, but that was the fascination: that sitting there, on that ugly green carpet—my father passed out on the couch, my mother fixing dinner, my brothers outside playing—what if I witnessed the dancing particles of static slowly cohere into shadowy but recognizable human forms emerging through a screen of fast-falling static snow, the uniform hissing now modulating in and out of a lopsided electromagnetic buzz, an eerie emission of sound swinging like a pendulum back and forth, closer and farther, before the signal collapsed and returned to a blizzard of static.

The UHF dial was a deceptively simple-looking but powerful tool which always promised the possibility of making contact with a world that transcended and transformed my own. It offered not an escape from my dingy, cramped working-class household of four boys, a housewife, and a frequently inebriated autoworker, but rather a mediation between that household and a geographic location both exotic and familiar. The UHF dial did not lift me out of my world into another but rather allowed me to encounter that other location through a fantasy space created by the electromagnetic traces delivered into my living room.

I recall the first time I ever watched cable television, a few years later, and the vague consternation I felt upon noticing that the UHF dial, only minimally utilized before, had now been rendered completely non-functional. The year was 1979. My oldest brother, then a teenager whose job at the bowling alley allowed him this luxury, had paid for a cable hook-up on the small black-and-white television he had received for Christmas and which sat in his makeshift basement room. If I remember correctly, my parents didn't even know about the cable at first, though he proudly gave my brothers and me a demonstration. He showed us the coaxial cable and explained that the signal came through it and not the air. Then he flipped the VHF knob and every channel displayed a picture, no static. "What about UHF?" I asked, grabbing the UHF dial. "What about channel 41 or channel 19?" I asked. It didn't receive channel 41 or any other UHF channels anymore because now channel 41 and channel 19 were cable channels on the VHF dial, the same shows as before only now with perfect reception. To me this innovation was a change that should have signaled to us all that something was out of kilter in the world, an echo of Samuel Morse's "What hath God wrought?" Television in the future, I now believe myself to have intuited quite despondently back then, would have no need for the UHF dial.

As long as my parents clung to their stubborn televisual asceticism—it would not be until the 1980s that my father finally embraced the idea of paying for television—I was able to continue fantasizing about receiving a signal from far beyond Kansas City, maybe from Des Moines or Maine or even from across the ocean. I imagined, too, how I would react when it finally happened. It would have been a sweet vindication for the repeated scoffing by my family at my insipid experiments, for my father's angry warnings to "stop that" or I would "wear out the dial." But it would also have been terrifying, an event something like that prototypical scene in the original Star Trek TV series. Lieutenant Uhura has been fiddling for hours with the controls of the huge video communication screen at the front of the bridge, Kirk checking with her repeatedly to no avail: "Have you got anything yet, Uhura?" Then, suddenly, after a few spurts of leftover static and zapping lines taking over the screen and then receding, the ominous face of the alien commander appears and delivers his ultimatum before they "lose him" again. I was sure that if I tuned something in on channel 47 or channel 58 I would have called out to my father, still passed out on the couch, or to my mother in the other room, but, like a child so scared that he screams but cannot make a sound, I would only have been able to mouth the words calling for them to come bear witness that we were actually receiving, indistinct and temporary though the signal may have been . . . TV Greenland!

The emotion aroused in me by this fantasy was a variety of the feeling of conceptual transcendence and pleasurable terror theorized in the 18th century by Kant and Burke under the term "sublime." Each thinker emphasized a different aspect of this one phenomenon. Kant in his *Critique of Judgment* emphasized that tendency of some objects or experiences to exceed our ability to conceptualize them concretely: we can easily picture the concept of "two" and maybe even "ten," but after that things start to get fuzzy and a unit like "five million light years" becomes utterly impossible to picture within the framework of our mental categories; the feeling such failure arouses is one aspect of the sublime. Burke's conception of the sublime did not contradict Kant's but examined the same phenomenon from a different perspective. He defined the sublime quite simply as the feeling of terror, but the bulk of his famous tract on the sublime investigated not terror per se but rather the odd fact that, while danger or pain in themselves are unpleasant, when we experience them at a safe distance, as in art, the feelings aroused are quite pleasurable.

Analog broadcast television aroused in me a feeling of the sublime, in both the Kantian and the Burkean senses, that I am convinced is absent in both analog television delivered by cable and digital television. The difference has nothing to do with the actual content of the shows. After all, many shows that were originally broadcast on analog television are now re-broadcast on cable or digital TV or available for viewing on *YouTube* or DVD with the same content—in some cases even additional content—found in the original versions. Nevertheless, when I revisit those shows in a format different from their original, or even watch new shows for that matter, the experience is much different. Nor can this difference, the sublime effect of analog broadcast television, consist in the fact that these shows were originally broadcast through the air from a station that may have been many miles away. Digital TV and satellite TV, after all, are both airborne transmission methods, and yet the crispness and stability of the images they reproduce seem somehow to belie the distance these images travel and renders the experience equivalent to just watching a DVD on a computer.

In the age of analog broadcasts, a certain aura was created on the screen by knowing that the successful reception of a program was at least in part the result of chance and, even more specifically, of the weather. Indeed, during a violent summer storm, reception might be severely impaired due to lightning or clouds or, after the storm had passed, a bent antenna on the roof, but the TV screen itself reflected this trauma, even kept a running, visual transcript of it. The picture would slowly start hissing and the colors would turn to black and white and start disintegrating into pixels. The result was a distorted but still visible space which stirred the imagination and could even inspire that feeling of pleasurable terror identified by Burke. Furthermore, the impairment of the transmission made me wonder how it all worked, how these components came together at those other times when the signal did arrive intact. No matter how long I thought about it, though, the parts always added up to more than their composite sum and I could never get, conceptually, from these now somewhat more isolated elements to their cooperation at other times in the form of a single picture on the screen. The very interference that digital broadcast today promises to eliminate, thus spurred me to assume an estranged relationship to my material world: analog television was a version of Heidegger's tool, the miracle of whose successful functioning we take for granted and only begin to appreciate and really start to ponder—though never fully understand—when the tool breaks down.

Granted, cable and digital TV, for all their reliability, sometimes go on the fritz, but when that happens the temporarily disarmed technology of digital does not invite our wonder or imagination to share its space with it. On the contrary, there is only a cutting out, the "cliff effect" of binary technology, whereby the screen simply loses any signal whatsoever and goes blue or, in the case of analog cable, goes to pure static. The Protean malleability of analog television static made possible my improbable hope of receiving a signal from beyond the reach of what it would have been reasonable to expect. If the signal could fade in and out in varying degrees of strength during a thunderstorm, that meant that such variability was always involved in any reception of a signal. In contrast to digital there was no "cliff" effect after which the signal simply dropped off. In a modern-day inversion of Zeno's paradox, any analog signal *always* arrived at my house because, even if there had been a point in space where the radio waves of a transmission simply stopped, I could always imagine a slightly weaker signal emerging out of the previous signal and carrying the transmission just a little bit farther, and so on. In fact, my TV was *already* receiving TV Greenland: My vision simply was not acute enough to detect the picture among the billions and billions of particles of snow. With digital, though, the signal does just seem to stop and fall over a cliff. On or off. Thus, during the interruption of a signal, the screen offers no representation of anything that would allow us to imagine that malleability of the image that, in broadcast television, by contrast, was such an important feature.

I can still remember vividly one particular instance of watching TV with my family, a rerun of a *Star Trek* episode on channel 41, when a thunderstorm hit in late summer, just after my mother had cleared the table in time to watch her favorite show. As darkness fell prematurely upon our neighborhood, the signal began to break up into pixels just at those most exciting moments in the plot: Kirk wrestling a brightly hued humanoid or the shuttle trying to make an emergency landing on the planet below. Sometimes, often in conjunction with a flash of lightning and the explosion of thunder, we would lose the signal almost, but never quite completely. It always came back, no matter how violent the storm, unless the electricity went out (a trauma that rendered our television "digital" quite against its will) or the antenna on the roof was bent. Thus, the sublime terror in the presence of a thunderstorm—that feeling in the back of my mind that, despite the odds, something violent could happen to me at any moment—was represented on the TV screen in the form of a fading and returning signal, and it was terrifying and pleasurable at the same time to experience both effects, the storm and the fluctuating signal, with my family. Part of the sublimity came from wondering whether that signal threatening to disappear entirely would reestablish itself—like a passenger on an airplane wondering whether the plane will recover from a sudden jolt of turbulence or whether instead this is "it." Then, as the dark skies were replaced by the peaceful, luminescent green of a freshly watered earth and as the crew of the *Enterprise* wrapped up their mission on yet another planet, so too did the signal come back gradually in all its clarity, showing only the faintest layer of static, just as in the air outside hovered only the trace of precipitation from a violent threat now passed. No such traces, neither of light nor of violent nature nor of the imagination, can be found in the digital alternation at the height of a storm between only a full signal and an empty blue screen.

Though the sublimity of static was most evident during a thunderstorm, it was not only or even primarily through bad weather that this unconscious of analog broadcast television made itself known. The static was always there, even when it couldn't be seen, just as our unconscious is always there. It permeated the UHF channels, but even on the VHF dial, in the days before remote control, there was that unused space between the network affiliated channels, a distance that had to be traveled like the highway we so anxiously wish away as our cars putter towards their destination. Sometimes, though, my attention might linger and I would wonder about whether channel 7 or channel 12 would look the same tomorrow or whether the next violent thunderstorm, while impairing the signal on other channels, might actually bring closer on these channels some signal from far away. This static was not only an ever-present canvas, a screen *on* which the images of TV shows took shape, but also a primordial pool *from* which these images emerged. When I changed the channel or turned off the TV, these images didn't just disappear, but rather they returned to their natural state, static, awaiting their resurrection at my command.

This fantasy space constituted by the static was so powerful that it invaded my own unconscious to a degree impossible with cable or digital technology. As a child my dreams about television were frequent and vivid. There were the pleasant nighttime visions of receiving right there in Lexington, Missouri a signal from Newfoundland or England or Greenland on channel 59 or channel 276 (such are the distortions of the dream work), as crisp and invigorating as a storm coming in off of the Denmark Strait. Surely I smiled in prolonged angelic slumber as images of Greenlandic children running through fields and springing over rustic fences played on a UHF station that I watched in my head. But there were also nightmares or, if not nightmares, at least the return of the televisual repressed.

In one dream my brother and I are sitting in the upstairs room of my grandmother's old house trying to tune something in on the static-filled screen of her television, no doubt a UHF station, when suddenly we realize that the television is not just a television but also a monitoring device. Instead of recognizable forms slowly emerging from the static, it is our images that are being captured by the static and transmitted to some nameless, faceless people watching us from somewhere far away, perhaps even Greenland. I turn to my brother and whisper, let's get out of here, and we open the door into the adjoining attic. We close the door behind us and crouch in the dark, hiding, though we both know that the television is still in the other room, still on and silently laughing at its power over us, a power to which we had been blind: how stupid we were to think, like the family in *Poltergeist*, that the static was just static and not a membrane of contact with another world, a door into the unconscious that opened in both directions.

To watch a broadcast of any show against the backdrop of this rich and complex space was an eerier, uncannier, and more sublime experience than watching those same shows or any other shows through the modern technologies of today. I recall, for example, the occasional viewings at school of the original *Letter People* program, a children's literacy program with puppets, in my second grade classroom in 1976. Like the viewings of a film, these broadcasts of educational TV shows were special occasions when the partition separating our classroom from the adjoining classroom was drawn back—these were the heady and experimental days of "open classroom" pedagogy—and a celebratory and communal atmosphere pervaded the room that now had twice as many students crammed into it, half of them sitting on the floor.

Letter People was developed and produced at the KETC public television studio in St. Louis between 1974 and 1976 and syndicated nationally. The broadcast that we watched originated from KCPT, Kansas City Public Television, channel 19, about 45 miles due west of Lexington. The radio waves that brought the show to us traveled unobstructed over the currents of the Missouri River and passed over the cool concrete of the playground, over the heads of children with inexcusably archaic haircuts and clashing plaid pants and striped shirts in 1970s patterns and colors, before finally reaching the antenna that shot up proudly from the roof of Leslie Bell Elementary, next to the flagpole the tallest structure on the school grounds.

The show was truly eerie, at times terrifying, and always sublime. Looking back now, I cannot help but wonder whether one of the minds behind the show's creation might not have been some eccentric German expressionist filmmaker, someone with an artistic vision like Murnau or Lang but who never gained the success that allowed for the realization of that vision. So, during the Nazi-era, instead of fleeing to Hollywood he flees to the adopted homeland of his great great uncles, the academic Hegelians and 48ers who had made St. Louis their home in the previous century. Then, in the early 1970s, just as he is about to pass into retirement and permanent obscurity, after a disappointing career of directing underappreciated public service announcements for a local public TV station, his big break comes and he is asked to write and maybe even also create the puppets for KETC's new show.

The letter people were not cute, cuddly and clean like *Sesame Street*'s Muppets. Everything about them, their gigantic facial features, their clothes, their voices, were grating and unsettling, and yet fascinating. What lent these characters most of their eeriness, though, were the dark spaces of the puppet studio they inhabited. Even when that space was lighted, as in the scenes that purportedly took place outside in Letter People Land, it was dark, heavy, and opaque, full of pixilated atoms and molecules which transmitted light and sound but which also slowed this light and sound down and made them droop towards Letter People earth. The unique properties of that space I now contend were not the product of a bitter old German expressionist but rather the result

68

of that unconscious backdrop of analog static upon which that space was created. That space made Mr. S's alliterative wordplay into screeching hyper-sibilants, a steady downpour of sheets of rain every time he spoke. It made Miss A's huge face, sprouting arms and legs, into a tableau vivant, forever stuck to the same piece of ground, even though it appeared to move about freely. The visual and auditory properties of that space, always threatening to fall apart into the static that was its foundation, made the letter people seem pitifully mortal, their material coherence always about to be compromised, rendering them a bundle of unrecognizable phonetic features, pure difference, lying on Letter People earth. When I watch these shows now on *YouTube*, though, that full, uneven space has flattened out into a one-dimensional empty space. The only threat that lurks in the background is that the picture itself, and not the space or the objects inhabiting it, will freeze up in suspended animation or disappear completely.

Another sublime television experience was Godzilla. My brothers and I derided the laughably fake monsters and urban sets as if we had disclosed a ruse that the filmmakers had taken great pains to conceal. Despite the poor production quality of the movies, though, Godzilla had a sublimity to him as he towered above toy skyscrapers set against a sky that was obviously confined to the inside of a studio but for that reason seemed, paradoxically, to extend into infinity. On dreary winter Saturday mornings, the frost dripping down the caulk on the side of the living room window, I would look out across Highway 13 and try to imagine where exactly the forest ended and how far it was to the Missouri River that I knew lay only a few miles to the west. In that landscape I would imagine Godzilla, now a real giant reptile and no longer a Japanese actor in a rubber suit, only his shoulders and head visible above the barren maples and oaks, far off in the distance but with every bouncing step sneaking up closer behind the Lafayette County welfare office, which faced our house. In this wooded fantasy-scape of my mind, Godzilla faded in and out of reality, materializing out of thin air and receding again (and not just suddenly there and suddenly gone). This imaginative capacity to bring Godzilla into existence in the woods near my house (and not just in a made-up space that existed only in my mind) was an effect of seeing the world through eyes trained by analog static, which showed me a world that could fade back and forth between here and somewhere else without ever being completely in one place or the other.

Disaster, not the improbable disaster of a giant reptile attacking our small town, but the disaster hinted at, without ever being explicitly named, by the Emergency Broadcast System test, was another sublime source of fascination for me as a child. Again I cannot help but feel that the sublimity through which I experienced my fear of an "actual emergency" would have been lessened if I had grown up in a world of digital or cable television.

The EBS test, especially the one broadcast on Kansas City's only independent station, KBMA, channel 41, seemed to produce such a chilling effect because of the low quality of its production. The image shown on the screen and the sounds that accompanied it, the beep and the voice, were not slickly produced with the aid of a computer. They didn't even seem like they were prerecorded, but rather felt like they were pulled together on the spot, each time anew. Watching it, I could almost sense the presence of the human beings who had created and were transmitting them. The announcer's voice sounded as if he had just run in from outside and was now speaking, muffled and barely comprehensible, on a megaphone, as if trying to control a crowd. Even the graphic was frightening, not because of what it showed, but because, like KBMA's "technical difficulties" sign, it looked like it was being held up manually in front of the camera; at times you

70

would swear it was shaking. As in *Letter People* there was a palpably heavy space in these spots, the result again of that unconscious backdrop of static, that made this suspected presence of human beings feel terrifyingly close and rendered the entire production uncanny and sublime. As a small child I dreaded the appearance of these spots—like nuclear war itself, they could come at any time—but my fear was mixed with the ecstasy of terror at the same time, and so, when the test would come on, rather than leaving, I would continue to watch but call my mother in from the other room.

As for the childhood quest that framed all of these briefer moments of sublime terror—the desire to see TV Greenland or its equivalent on my TV screen—I can honestly assert, in bold defiance of digital logic, that I neither did nor did not succeed. There was that day, which must have been in the late '70s, 1979 or maybe 1980, when I was old enough to stay home alone sick but before we moved into a larger and nicer house on the edge of town, fully equipped with cable and two television sets with remote controls and no UHF dials. I remember sitting in front of the TV set tuning the UHF dial and then gradually bringing before my eyes a channel in the 60s, maybe channel 67. I tried desperately to turn the dark purple space cut by horizontal lines into a recognizable transmission. The audio signal was distorted just enough that I could still recognize it as human speech but could not make out any of the words. The picture kept breaking up into horizontal lines. I had learned that the appropriate response to a distorted signal was to adjust the tiny white "horiz." knob on the back of the set, though I now had the growing hunch that, like its "vert." counterpart, it could only help adjust regular channels, the ones we usually received clearly. All it could provide me with now was the illusion of exerting more control over one of the many unknown variables involved in my Quixotic quest.

As it turned out, it was not by turning any knobs but simply by waiting patiently that the signal started coming in more clearly and became the recognizable but still veiled image of a talk show, men dressed in suits and a woman in a dress, sitting on one side of a stage, the host standing on the other side, the cameras cutting back and forth between them. They all appeared on the screen as shadowy humanoids with glowing electrified outlines that distinguished their bodies from the black nebulous space behind them. These electrified outlines were auras that moved when the bodies of the people moved. Because the people were electromagnetic shadows, they seemed to be mocking my own corporeality. Then the signal faded back out, going almost to pure static, but then hanging on and coming back strong again, like the lights in a small apartment experiencing a brownout, fading slowly in and out.

Looking back now I still don't know what that show was or where it came from. It could have been a news show, a religious show, or even a game show. I remember flipping through all the VHF channels to make sure it wasn't just a duplication of another channel. I knew all the channels listed in the Kansas City area *TV Guide* backwards and forwards as well as their places of origin. This was no channel 2 from St. Joseph or even channel 27 from Topeka. It wasn't any station from Western Missouri or Eastern Kansas, It was something new and different. I was confident that in time I would be able to identify it.

Of course, as precipitously as this new channel—from Omaha or Springfield or Jefferson City, or from somewhere even farther away—had come in, it was gone again, and I never got it back. This event neither did nor did not happen, I assert, because I cannot remember whether the event occurred in reality or in a dream. If it was a dream, I can't even remember if the dream took place around the same time as the event it depicted or whether I dreamt it much later, a nostalgic wish-fulfillment and a symbolic closure to my fantasy life in the old house and the quest that framed so much of it. A letting go of childhood fantasy but also thereby a voluntary narrowing of my imagination.

In his famous essay, "The Significance of the Frontier in American History," Frederick Jackson Turner argued that the closing of the American frontier in the 19th century represented a narrowing in the range of feeling and imaginative capacity of all Americans. There seems to be a similar restriction brought about by the end of analog broadcast television. Just as the end of Westward settlement sapped our imagination by transforming the wide-open spaces of the West into pure myth, so now does the closing off of the broad expanses of the television spectrum, and its consequent drift into a nostalgic afterlife, signal a similar restriction on our ability to imagine ourselves as historically or even technologically different. From now on, culture, already programmed and packaged by national or even international corporations in an increasingly rational and cost-effective manner, will tend towards a binary system of on or off, a clear, lifeless full signal or a clear, lifeless, empty screen. The railroad tracks have been laid, so to speak, the highways built, the inefficient streetcars banned, and the animals that once roamed free and spurred the imagination, even if only as a myth of what could never really be, have all been fenced in. From now on, we will be able to look forward only to the increasingly faster and more efficient transfer of goods and services across the now well-established routes of the electromagnetic spectrum, once upon a time washed over by the murky yet fertile swamps and grasslands of UHF static.

But is not this loss of an intangible fantasy space made up for by the efficiency of transmission and even increase in content that digitally broadcast television represents? Just as at the turn of the 20th century, Turner pointed out, American cities were beginning to build up, in the form of skyscrapers, rather than out, towards the Pacific Ocean, so now, we are told, does digital broadcasting offer the ability to do more with less. Digital technology allows TV stations to broadcast three separate programs using a bandwidth significantly smaller than that taken up by a single analog channel. But does digital television offer more or just the appearance of more? Is it not the same seemingly unlimited variety that we now encounter everywhere from the grocery store aisle to the Internet, a variety that we are told signifies our freedom, but in fact turns out to be a reduplicating chain of cereal boxes and reality TV shows only minimally and superficially different from one another?

In that same childhood house on Highway 13, across from the welfare office and the forest in which Godzilla was always about to take shape, my older brothers used to perform a trick on our dial telephone. When my oldest brother, the one who a few years later would first introduce cable into our household, asked me one day, "Do you want to hear Frankenstein's heartbeat?" the fact that I didn't say yes or no did not stop him from showing me. He lifted up the phone and, after a hopelessly indecipherable combination of half-dials and clicks of the metal hook, he put the phone to my ear, a mischievous smirk on his face that I was starting to construe as evil, and a regular rhythm of plodding thumps traveled into my ear. He laughed. I cried from mortal terror.

In the American child's future, there will be no more Frankenstein's heartbeats, no more records spun backwards to try to hear a hidden message, no more classroom films melting on the screen and slowly opening up a womb that beckons the children sitting in the dark to enter into another dimension. And no more static on the television screen, no space in which the little girl in *Poltergeist* learns to see a world more primal than the one offered her by suburbia. No longer will children be terrified by these unconscious "ghosts," the power of the sublime, that inhabited analog technology. If fear can be aroused and the imagination stirred by digital media, from now on it is only by the overt content of these media, programmed and planned out carefully by marketing experts—the overwrought and unspectacular roar of THX sound or the saccharine and easy cleverness of Pixar animation—and no longer by any unconscious elements that affect us without our understanding, at the time anyway, how or why. TV Greenland will be either fully available on the Internet or fully absent. We need to stop and consider, and perhaps even mourn, the immense loss this represents.

On June 12th, 2009, we took a leap into a future from which, as with all movements into the future, whether in the form of small steps or giant leaps, there is no turning back. We are now at home in a culture that will soon be either fully on or fully off, with increasingly little space in between for variation or for the play of unconscious fantasy. Some will respond that this unconscious space of fantasy, the quirks and material excess that characterized analog technology, can be rediscovered in digital technology, if only we look hard enough. I hope, for the sake of our need to imagine ourselves neither fully in nor fully outside of the present, that they are right. As for me, as for now, when I watch the frozen up image from a scratched DVD stuck in an immovable digital loop, my fantasy is not aroused; I see rather only the endless repetition of the same.

Jeannine Hall Gailey

Snow White's Near Miss

Hey this place looks dangerous she said, pulling her ebony
hair around her like a shining veil. The alleyway glowered
with malice. You'll be fine he said. See that tiny shack in the
distance? If you work as a maid I'm sure they'll pay you.
She looked doubtful, pouting in the moonlight. He was,
after all, carrying an axe. All these huntsman are the same,
she thought, promising candy and nosegays, planning to cut
out your heart. There was a dead deer on the tracks, its one
good eye still open and gazing at the stars. Thump-thump,
called the deer heart in the darkness. He took it with him
back to the castle inside a velvet sack. It was a messy job.
Girl or deer, you never quite get used to the cracking of
bones, the outpour of gore, even after all these years of
killing, of blood on your hands.

JEANNINE HALL GAILEY

The Little Mermaid Has No Regrets

In the end, I wanted to wake up sea foam.
I didn't want these legs anymore, that carry me
uselessly from house to house, searching for lost love.
I wore dresses that covered up the pale lengths,
in sea greens and azure blues, wove seashells into hair
and sang on a rock. None of it did any good.

Once, I would have died for you. I changed, I did,
and all for just one kiss, one touch. Should it have burned
so much? I miss cool scales, the constant wet embrace,
the skittering across tips of tsunami. While you
were out catching fish, with your tangled nets,
I was watching, wishing for a different body, one to entangle you.

It never did me any good. So I will wait for the ocean's promise:
that once again I will end up on this beach, disintegrate,
spatter away into the essences of salt, sand, earth.
A waste of skin and scale, but at least once again
I will be part of the dance, the maternal water
carrying me home.

ERIC MORROW

The Rise of the Nerd

Alea iacta est.
Translation: *"The die is cast."*
—Julius Caesar, 49 BC

I rolled a 20! Double damage!
—The Dead Alewives Watchtower,[1] 1996

Our story starts in a dark room. Our hero, such as he is, finds himself sitting at the corner of a large table. In the dim light of a few meager light bulbs, the dark slab of wood might appear as an altar, the bags of chips and cans of soda offerings to some unnamed god. The faces of his companions are cast dark and brooding in the pale light of the bulbs dotting the walls of the kitchen. The surface of the table is nearly covered by a large grid lined map and bits of spiral notebook parchment scribbled with esoteric writings and cryptic numbers. One man, separated from the others by an elaborately decorated cardboard screen, turns his gaze on our hero.

"Alright Eric. Sorry, I mean Healy, it's your turn. What do you do?"

There is a slight pause. The hero glances across the tabletop battlefield, takes a deep breath and finally says "Okay, I'm gonna punch the big guy—With my mind."

"What?"

"I cast Mental Blast at the leader."

"Oh, cool. Okay, give me a roll."

---

[1] Improvisational comedy troupe from Milwaukee, Wisconsin. Quote from the sequel to their famous "Dungeons and Dragons" skit.

78

With a slow, deliberate motion our hero reaches forward and slightly disturbs the organized pile of stones in front of him. He picks the icosahedron, the one with twenty sides, the d20[2]. He grips it gently between his thumb and pointer finger, its smooth green facets glinting in the light, before cupping it gently in the palm of his hand. He gives it a few quick shakes, whispers a prayer, and casts the die, and with it his character's destiny, across the table...

Nerd History: For Dummies

Many readers will find the terminology used in this text quite incomprehensible. This is not due to any inherent lack of intelligence on the part of the reader. It merely illustrates the vast cultural gulf between nerds and the rest of society. This schism may have been around since the beginning of time, but it was not until relatively recently that a label was attached it.

In 1950 author Theodor Geisel, known to most as Dr. Seuss, coined the word "nerd" in his book *If I Ran the Zoo*. A year later the magazine *Newsweek* defined the term as a synonym for "a drip" or "a square"(*Newsweek*). By the 1970s the word was being used as a pejorative term for any intellectual, "bookish," or socially awkward individual. The word gained popularity as an insult thanks to popular television shows such as *Happy Days*.

Then came the 1980s, and with it came the first computers and *Revenge of the Nerds* and the beginnings of the so-called "nerd pride movement" of the '90s. Suddenly there was an outlet for individuals of the "nerd persuasion" to find some of the limelight. It seemed as though the proverbial

---

[2] A 20-sided die, the most common type used in paper and pencil role playing games.

pendulum had swung in favor of the nerds. Only one question remained, had it swung too far?

Brief Character Description

Heroes aren't born, they're made. The hero of our story, such as he is, was made sporadically over the course of twenty-one years. His nature is composite and his design chaotic. When he was a child, he would glue himself to the television for each new episode of the Power Rangers[3]. The following day he would battle his three sisters for the rights to use the same television to watch nature documentaries about exotic sea life and educational programs about Roman history and Astronomy.

A brief foray into the realm of team sports began and ended abruptly with a little league soccer team. In his second year his team mates, all displaying the heraldry of "The Red Lightning Bolts" began a merciless campaign, chiding his lack of co-ordination and control on the field. Their favorite taunt was to promise to "put him in a body bag"[4] by the end of practice. He would never willingly participate in the realm of team sports again.

His academic life was more successful. By the age of twelve he was in at least the 98th percentile of every standardized test except spelling and grammar in which he only ranked in the 95th. The entirety of his school career culminated in a 4.1 GPA and a full ride academic scholarship to the one college he applied to. Throughout middle and high school, his peers either mocked him for taking honors courses or despised him for maintaining high grades with minimal effort or studying. His social life will consisted of lonely

---

[3] Long-running American television show and marketing franchise. Borrowed much of its footage from the Japanese television show *Super Sentai*.

[4] According to recent sources, this phrase was most likely taken from watching wrestling on television. Not the real kind. The fake kind. With the scripts.

weekends playing computer games and painting models. His first kiss happened at age nineteen. At the time that this tale was chronicled, the hero had not been on a single date.

His hobbies include tabletop war games and pen-and-paper role playing games. His favorite television shows include *Firefly*[5], *Dr. Who*[6], and *QI*[7]. He has personally tracked down and watched every episode of Monty Python's[8] Flying Circus[9]. On slow nights he will surf the internet for interesting facts and information, a habit that has more than once led to impromptu self-led math lessons about infinite probability and harmonic averages. He enjoys comic books but prefers to read them when the anthologies come out so that the story is uninterrupted.

His hobbies and inclinations are what first led him to his current endeavor. He is currently filming a local independent movie. The movie is an adventure film about a group of LARPers[10]. The hero of this story is not the hero in the movie. However, both of these heroes are true nerds, both are good friends, and neither of the heroes gets the girl at the end of his story.

Involuntary Celibacy

It is four weeks before filming officially begins, and our hero, such as he is, is finally spending the night at a girl's house. He

---

[5] American "space western" television show created by Joss Whedon. Ran for one season before Fox ruined it.

[6] British science fiction television show about a time traveling adventurer. Began in 1963 and is still in production.

[7] British quiz show. QI stands for "Quite Interesting." The show is so impossibly difficult that contestants are rewarded for interesting answers rather than correct ones.

[8] British sketch comedy troupe that began work in the 1960's.

[9] The television show started by the eponymous sketch comedy troupe in the 1960's. It's way better than their movies.

[10] "Live Action Role Players"

spends the majority of the evening regaling tales of rehearsals and classes, and even takes the time to give a brief explanation of why light can't escape a black hole, a concept he learned about from his own personal research. For the most part his companion is silent, only giggling from time to time. At one point in the conversation she takes an opportunity to comment on his story.

". . . pansy." That's what she calls him. She says it lightly, almost playfully, but with full conviction and sincerity. Again, she giggles, but this time the hero detects no mirth, only condescension. It is clear that she views him not with lust or pleasure, but pity.

Eventually she reaches over and turns out the light. He read somewhere that the average American falls asleep in about eleven minutes. He isn't sure if he sleeps at all. He just lies there for seven hours without moving. Nothing happens. All he hears for seven hours is an insult and a giggle ringing in his ears.

"All Your Base Are Belong To Us"[11]

In 1997, *Harry Potter and the Philosopher's Stone* by J.K. Rowling was released in the U.K. There were five hundred books in the first printing. Ten years later, in 2007, *Harry Potter and the Deathly Hallows* was released. It sold almost 11 million copies worldwide in the first 24-hours (BBC). Across the globe millions of eager readers dressed up in pointy hats and brightly colored cloaks and flocked to their local book stores to attend release parties and events. Nobody can deny that it was one of the great cultural phenomena of the past century.

---

[11] Text from a poorly translated version of the Japanese video game "Zero Wing." Became an internet meme in 2000.

One important fact to note, in regards to nerd culture, is that many of the individuals attending these events labeled themselves as "true Harry Potter nerds." Most of them were nothing of the sort. Teenagers wearing black trash bags tied off-center around their necks waving shiny ten-cent pencils with bright five pointed stars capping the erasers hardly qualify as a blip on the nerd radar. Being a nerd takes work. The 53-year-old woman wearing the emerald cape with the golden silk lining, holding the hand-crafted replica wand made from a willow tree and sporting unicorn pendants and laurel leaf bracelets made of sterling silver, is the only one who can truly claim to be a Harry Potter nerd.

At some point in the last twenty years, the majority of the population decided that being different was being cool. Apparently irony has become hip. This has led to the creation of groups of people like casual nerds, metro-sexuals, hipsters, and white rappers (a trend this author finds both disturbing and hilarious). Vast hordes of shallow husks realized that they could reap the benefits of these lifestyles without paying the costs.

The truest definition of "nerd" is an individual who is a social outcast, unwilling or unable to conform to popular trends. Over the years the word has, like a snowball rolling down a mountain, accumulated connotations, both good and bad. Amongst the connotations are intelligence, a pre-occupation with fantasy and science fiction, social awkwardness, lack of aggression or charisma, and an inability to attract the opposite sex. However, in the same span of time a culture has grown up around the word, refined by scorn and solitude, to become something unique and individual. Nobody can take that away, not even for the night of a Harry Potter release.

This is a nerd's world. You're only visiting.

You Do Not Choose the Weapon,
The Weapon Chooses You.

It is a chilly summer afternoon on the second day of filming. Our hero, such as he is, stands on the field of battle. Soft, claylike Missouri mud lies beneath a thin layer of grass under the trees our hero is defending. Around him stand his allies, stout men and women all. Each of them wields their weapons like pros, veterans of a hundred battles now long past. Together they stand in defense of their tiny copse of trees. Each one knows his or her part in what his to come. The tanks[12], the archers, and our hero, the healer.

He holds a spear. Six feet of reinforced bamboo, weighted on one end, covered with black tape and tipped with a rectangular piece of foam the length of his forearm. It is a boffer[13], and it outweighs his usual armament by an easy half-stone[14].

Without warning the enemy attacks. One of our hero's comrades falls to a well placed projectile to the chest: an arrow shaft tipped with a tennis ball. Our hero takes a single step and feels a sharp pain lance through his side. He glances down in time to see a javelin bounce off the boniest part of his hip. It was one of the new ones, not yet properly broken in, and the foam on the tip hurts almost as much as if it hadn't been there at all. According to the rules, our hero falls to one knee, injured, but not out.

Our hero continues to his objective, the comrade who was cut down by a distant archer. Upon reaching his ally, he says the words. After a ten second cast time, the man stands up, grabs his boffer, smiles and suddenly points. Our hero

---

[12] A common combat role in role playing parties. The tank's job is to draw attacks and defend party members.

[13] A mock weapon used in Live Action Role Playing. Often made of PVC pipe or wood covered with foam.

[14] Archaic form of measuring weight. A stone is equal to 20 lbs.

turns, barely blocking the strike of a spear just as long and heavy as his own. He is unprepared for the second strike, and the force of the impact thrusts his own spear out of his hands. Fifteen pounds of reinforced bamboo strike our hero just beside his eye. It is a glancing blow that leaves him stunned.

After a few seconds the hero stands and shouts "Hold!"

All around him the clamor of battle is silenced. According to the rules, when someone shouts hold, everyone stops, because someone is hurt. The hero, thankful for a few moments of respite to gain his bearings once more, is about to shout "lay on" when he hears a familiar voice in the background.

"Oh my God! Dude, you're bleeding!"

Our hero touches his temple, a single dot of blood is left on his finger. Only when he sees the pictures later does he understand. The dot of blood has come from a thin trickle that is now dripping from the edge of his jaw, the drops landing in almost the exact spot on his jeans where a green and purple bruise already throbs, a souvenir from a foam javelin.

The owner of the familiar voice walks over, holding a camera. He snaps a picture before the "medics" in the vicinity can begin their work.

"Well, 'Pastor Healy.' Second day of filming and you've already shed blood for this movie. Think you're ready for the big time?"

"No," replies the hero. "Not until I can use my boffer to make someone other than myself bleed." Those around him laugh, but our hero doesn't. Beaten up by teenagers holding foam swords. Cut himself with a stick of wood. Our hero feels anything but ready.

Foam Sword Soldier—
What I Learned From Training

The first thing you learn is to attack the man not the sword. Flesh, not foam. If it doesn't feel pain, you have the wrong target. The second thing you learn is how much foam can hurt. A bruised collar bone and a bloody nose teach valuable lessons about reflexes and blocking.

The third thing you learn is that she is laughing at you, not with you.

The fourth thing you learn is wear jeans, not shorts. Rocky soil bloodies knees quicker than you might think, and new players spend most of their time as the kneeling wounded. The fifth thing you learn is how to cheat, and the sixth is that you are the only one who isn't. The next thing you learn is that one thing is missing from these simulated battles: fear. You learn that shields are cheap, healers are weak, and role playing is better on paper.

You learn that girls only dig scars that didn't come from foam swords, and that they say things like *I like nerds* and *I like zoos* in almost exactly the same way. You learn that no matter how many spells you know in character or how good you are with a staff, you will never impress her as much as a full grown beard, a crushed pack of cigarettes, and a '67 Mustang.

The last thing you learn, foam sword in hand, is that you've learned more than anyone else on the field.

A Telling of Tales

It is two in the afternoon on the first day of filming. The entire cast and crew has been crammed into a small living room. Before they start filming, the directors ask everyone the same question: Why do you want to do this movie? The last person to answer the question is our hero, such as he is. He speaks slowly, deliberately. He has weighed his words carefully, weeded out his tendency to ramble. He picks bits of fuzz out of the cream shag carpet he is sitting on.

"There are a lot of things in my life I'm not happy about. There are a lot of things I wish I could change. I wish I was stronger, faster, better looking. I wish I didn't have to defend the things I do or like just because some jock thinks it's weird. But I have always been a nerd. I have never, and will never, apologize for it. It isn't what I do. It's who I am. It's the one part of me I'm proud of, and if I have to deal with the rest of it then fine. I'm a nerd, and I'm not alone."

The director smiles, just with the corners of his mouth, but he smiles. He only had one thing to say to that. "You had me at hello."

Works Cited

Geisel, Theodor Seuss. *If I Ran the Zoo*. New York: Random House Books for Young Readers, 1950. Print.
Newsweek. October 8, 1951:16. Print.
"Harry Potter Finale Sales Hit 11 m." *BBC.com*. BBC, 23 July 2007. Web. 03 May 2010.

PETE DUVAL

The World to Come

Vera looked about my age, mid-forties, but the gag around the diner was she wouldn't be born for another 200 years. The other regulars ribbed me: *Talk about robbing the cradle, RJ!* Slow mornings, we'd ask her about the world to come. How different would it be?

"I don't want to depress you," she'd say, pouring coffee, her soft brown eyes grown suddenly forlorn and weary.

That bad? we'd play along. Wasn't this America?

She said we didn't know how lucky we had it, how we took for granted "this world of chance textures and complexity and unexpected joy." She could set the regulars reeling on their stools, laughing. Once, she took it too far, holding forth about the coming "digital apotheosis," after which the essence of a person could be "rendered like hog fat into clean streams of information." Then she broke us up again with a crack about how hard time travel was on one's command of verb tense. She was easy on the eyes. As far as I was concerned, she could talk forever.

"Hey, Vera," someone yelled, "when you go back, take RJ with you."

Vera fixed me with one of her sexy looks. "I would if I could, RJ." But hadn't I heard? Anymore, she could only go one way, further into the past, and anyway she was more than happy in the here and now. She loved her diner. She loved watching customers sop up egg yolks with a folded triangle of wheat toast. When their eyes came alive with that first sip of coffee, so did hers. They didn't—they *wouldn't*—have coffee like that in the future. We raised our cups with a cheer. It *was* great coffee.

The night of our first date, after she'd sent the dishwasher home early and we were sitting on the same side of the corner booth, I was nervous. The moment had arrived. And what did I do? I fell back on the running joke. "How about the truth, Vera?" She cupped my jaw in her soft damp palm and brushed my cheek with her lips. I could smell the special—honey-glazed ham.

"You think you can handle the truth?"

It had been awhile for me, with a woman. And the details of my departure from teaching, I won't go into. Suffice it to say, tenure is a two-sided coin. Be careful what you wish for.

"I *know* I can, Vera. Lay it on me."

She pulled back, her eyes holding mine firm. "Maybe you can."

Lay it on me, she did. With a stack of napkins and a green felt-tipped pen, she began with an overview of General and Special Relativity, how position and time were *intimately involuted*. The movies had dumbed it down. The issue wasn't the *when*; the *when* was easy. It was all about the *where*. She bulleted out the eight motions of the earth—from tectonics to galactic rotation—then she smiled and sipped her coffee. She didn't want to brag, but she'd solved the problem herself—or *would* solve it. Time travel was at least a two-stage process. Sometimes you had to move forward to rendezvous with the same position you were in in the present. The rest was easy. "Does that make sense?" She slid her hand from my knee to my thigh.

I'd always been as big a fan of imaginative speculation as the next guy. But Vera was firing on cylinders I'd never even known she had. She was shining now.

Locate your Return Iteration Point—she seemed as proud of the term as she was of inventing the technology that had necessitated it—and you could get wherever, and *whenever,* you wanted to go. One catch: to hit your RIP, you needed *bidirectional capabilities.*

"And you have only unidirectional capacity now."

She winked. "Oh, RJ, you remembered." But there were much worse fates than living out your life in the Late Analogue Era, she said. When I pressed her for an example, she smoothed her warm fingers over the back of my neck and pulled me closer. Here was a woman who knew what she wanted. "'Overshooting the Interval,' for one."

I mouthed the phrase.

Go *too* far in either direction, forward or back, and you could skid beyond the singularity points at the beginning or end of the universe.

"That's gotta hurt," I said.

Vera fixed me with a hard and withering gaze. "You don't believe me, do you?" So I leaned in finally and kissed her. But her lips didn't move, and she tasted a bit sour, and when I opened my eyes, hers were already open, and unblinking. "You don't," she said. "I can see that."

"Vera, this is RJ, your biggest fan." Could she see her way to cutting me a break? After all, I was still living in the old world.

"Come with me," she said, shooing me out of the booth. She dragged me by the wrist under the counter gate near the register and back through the kitchen, past the heat still rising in waves above the stainless steel grills. She snapped off the fluorescents overhead. As we shuffled along a narrow hallway, the smell of bleach rushed in as though to overwhelm us in the darkness. "RJ," she said, her hand on the door to the back alley. "You have to promise me—"

"Come now, Vera. How long have we known each other?"

We stood before a battered receptacle the size of a coffin. Something to dump spent Frialator grease into. "Open up," she whispered. I stepped forward. From under the black-

90

ened lid a soft light like ocean phosphorescence was leaking. I wasn't one to refuse an order, not from a woman like Vera, not at this late date in my life. I did as she asked. I lifted the lid. But just before, I saw in her smile something new—as though the light was coming from her wise and beautiful face. She waited for the truth to blossom in me. She was nothing if not patient. "Now give me a hand here," she said, and we lifted a gray plastic garbage can of diner slop to the lip of the portal, then watched as the day's waste tumbled forth to bloat and spiral silently into the vacuum of space, the stars like salt spilled on dense black velvet.

II. Direct from Moon City

Rebecca James

Worms

My cat had tapeworms.
I found dry dead ones
like grains of rice in her fur.
And then, once, a live one—
translucent white, bunching up
then stretching out to inch its way.
My husband forced a blue pill
between the cat's clenching teeth.

Then I dreamed I had worms.
I coughed them up
and they sprang from cysts on my back:
black, millipedey worms,
white worms as long as shoelaces,
orange worms like cooked carrots.

I trudged through the apartment, quietly screaming.
My husband paced, solemn, behind me,
stooping to pick up worms by one end
and zipping them into plastic bags.

Rebecca James

Ghosts

Last night, my grandmother and great-grandmother
stood holding hands on my porch.
The younger dead twenty years,
the elder, twenty days.

My grandmother wore a crinoline,
a white satin bustier,
blush the color of roses too far-blown.
Half-dressed for her first wedding.

My great-grandmother dressed for her husband's funeral—
pale blue suit, ruffle-neck blouse,
turquoise and silver brooch.
She loved him for thirty more years,
ignoring the men who marveled at her exquisite cheekbones,
her hat-shielded skin resisting a wrinkle.

Peeking through the blinds and seeing them there,
I locked the bathroom door,
huddled in the bathtub.

They have walked Texas,
Oklahoma, Arkansas, Tennessee.
They began in New Mexico,
the land of my mother's childhood enchantment,
searching the skeletal windmill
where she and her cousins performed Rapunzel.

They caressed blooms in her old Nashville garden,
gone to seed and crabgrass.

And now they have trailed the scent to North Carolina,
crossing sandhill fields of goats and horses.
Mama is standing on her manicured Charlotte lawn
wearing rosebud pajamas, beckoning.
They have not seen her yet,
but will turn back toward her when they reach the coast.

Their pin-curls barely rustle in the breeze.
Will they take me first, always daughter before mother?
I want to go to them, take on the auburn hair,
green eyes, pale skin.
I wait, biting my knee in my porcelain cradle.

Eric Pervukhin

Playing Cards

Playing Card
The Banner of Parrots
Intaglio

Playing Card
The One of Batons
Intaglio

Playing Card
Two of Flowers
Intaglio

Playing Card
Four of Quadupeds
Intaglio

Playing Card
Five of Acorns
Intaglio

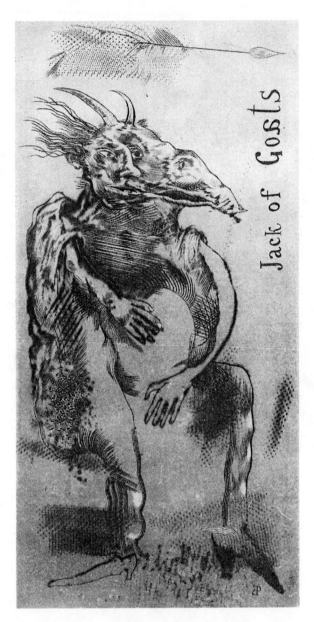

Playing Card
Jack of Goats
Intaglio

Playing Card
Trump Knave of Lions and Bears
Intaglio

Playing Card
Queen of Wild Men
Intaglio

Julie Platt

When I Played Indian

There's a small museum in the heart of the city of Pittsburgh. Inside are detailed models of battles: tiny British and French soldiers, tiny Indians with painted bodies in breechcloths, leggings. Tiny forts. Tiny cannons. Tiny death. Tiny wisps of cotton puff out of tiny muskets—stilled, forever—trying to drift upward into the tiny, tiny sky.

The workers at this museum wipe the glass that encloses the models and catalog the numbers on the guns and the cannonballs. They write stories for the museum newsletter. They stamp prices on the books in the gift shop, books like *Mary Jemison: White Woman of the Seneca* for $14.95, and *Crucible of War* for $28.50. Like any other museum, this one is focused on preservation, recreation, display. It's all about history, and about making it "come alive" again. As if history were dead.

In western Pennsylvania, the Allegheny and the Monongahela rivers flow into the Ohio, a massive tributary that continues west to join the Mississippi. The Allegheny and the Mon straddle a triangle of public parkland. Sunk into the green grass of Point State Park is a stone outline marking the original dimensions and the approximate location of Fort Duquesne, its four walls and diamond-shaped redoubts written permanently into the land. A minute's walk from the stone outline is the Blockhouse, an iron-black monolith of stone. It's the only intact remainder of Fort Pitt, which was built next to Fort Duquesne after the French destroyed and abandoned it. The Blockhouse is fenced off from the general public and guarded by a shiny D.A.R. plaque. Across the park path, built into the side of a hill that was once Fort Pitt's Monongahela bastion, is the Fort Pitt Museum. All of these structures are dwarfed by the relative largeness of the parkland they sit on, and the park is dwarfed further still by the city that sits at its edge, watching it. This city, Pittsburgh, is the city I am from. The Fort Pitt Museum is where I worked for one summer. These stone markers are images—maybe echoes, maybe bones—of the French and Indian War.

I knew little about the war when I began working at the museum. The week that I started, the staff was a flurry of breathless activity to prepare for Pioneer Days, an annual festival open to the public. I showed up at 6:30 on Saturday morning to set up tables, to make and hang signs, and to help welcome the re-enactors. They arrived half-dressed in wool breeches and heavy-metal band T-shirts, loaded down with wooden chests and bundles of linen. Some of them were employees of the museum's preservation society and sat on its board of directors, but many of them didn't get paid at all. They just showed up. As the festival opened to the public a 10 a.m., everything "modern" was hustled under piles of blankets and into corners of tents, and the re-enactors completed their dress. Some the re-enactors played British, in red and blue uniforms, the same shades of red and blue as their flag. Some played French, dressed in elegant coats of cream white and slate blue. And some of the re-enactors played Indian.

What is an Indian? Maybe most of us think we know. Maybe we picture someone tall and sober, wearing feathers and buckskins and turquoise jewelry. Maybe we've seen paintings of people who look like this. Maybe we've dressed as Indians for Halloween, or for the Boy Scouts or the Campfire Girls. Maybe we know someone who's "Indian." Maybe some of us bristle at the word Indian, and correct it to "Native American." Maybe some of us feel the straps of our white guilt cutting into us when we hear the word, when we

106

see the image in our minds. I am white, and I know myself in opposition. I am not an Indian, nor an American Indian, nor a Native American, nor Shawnee, nor Cherokee, nor Lenni Lenape, nor Choctaw, nor any names remembered or lost. Gerald Vizenor notes that "the Indian was an occidental invention that became a bankable simulation; the word has no referent in tribal languages or cultures" (11). Maybe some of us feel that we understand that, that "Indian" is a construction. But Vizenor continues: "the Indian is the simulation of [that] absence, an unreal name" (14). Indian. Created from minds intent on building binaries, filling boxes and books and museums, perhaps.

During my break from working Pioneer Days, I walked around gawking at the re-enactors. Farthest away from the museum was the Indian camp. Instead of erecting precise geometric tents like the British and French regiments and their camp followers, they spread blankets and skins neatly on the ground, and stood or sat, gazing at the crowd, waiting ambivalently to converse with the public. I nearly jumped out of my skin when a man painted pitch-black from head to toe called my name. It was David, one of my museum co-workers, dressed in a black wool breech-cloth and leggings, and a shapeless linen shirt with ruffles at the neck. His face was painted black, with red lightening bolts down either side.

"Are you having fun?" he asked.

"Are you?" I replied.

"We always have fun." The rest of the Indians—men and women, all adults—chuckled in agreement. "You should come play with us, next weekend, at the festival at North Park."

And so I discovered that even though Pioneer Days had ended, the re-enacting season had just begun. It was bigger than a few days at one museum. It was as big as the whole of the Ohio River Valley, as big as the whole country.

Re-enacting is essentially a performance, a drama, a play. You wouldn't think of it as the kind of play you sit quietly in a theater to see, although it's very much the same. The actors leave their modern things and modern selves behind the curtains, and they walk out with new faces to meet the audience. If they have to break character, they do so in the pockets of darkness and silence that surround the audience, for the audience moves through this play even as the play moves through the audience. The stage is the land—isn't the land the stage for every play? The script is history.

What does it mean to play Indian in present-day America? To discover the answer, it's important to look at where American records of playing Indian began—with the Boston Tea Party, where colonists angered by British tax laws donned blankets, feathers and paint and tossed chests of tea into the harbor. In *Playing Indian*, historian and critic Philip J. Deloria explains that "playing Indian is a persistent tradition in American culture, stretching from the very instant of the national big bang into an ever-expanding present and future. It is, however, a tradition with limitations. Not surprisingly, these cling tightly to the contours of power" (7). White American men have been the ones who played Indian the most, and "they have been the primary claimants of an American cultural logic that has demanded the formation and performance of national identities" (Deloria 7).

When the play is the French and Indian War, it's particularly difficult for those re-enactors who play Indian to find an accurate script. History is filled with rich descriptions of the white colonists, the ones who held the printing presses. Whites wrote the physicality and materiality of the natives, and these are often the only kinds of descriptions of native people available to the re-enactors. So the men and women who play Indian focus on reproducing their materiality as accurately as possible. Some of the players Deloria examines are object hobbyists, those whites who revered the materials and crafts associated with the Indian. He explains that "the object hobbyists envisioned an antimodern, exterior Indian Other, one that logically fit into the cluster of ideas that accompanied social Darwinism . . . for object hobbyists, the redemptive value of Indians lay not in actual people, but in the artifacts they had once produced in a more authentic stage of existence" (137). The re-enactors I knew showed a great deal of dedication to their hobby, even if their wives, husbands, children and friends didn't show much interest. Away from the camp, the lives of these Indian players were normal, suburban. But they hungered for their playtime. They were echoes of some of the earliest American Indian players, the white celebrants of the Boston Tea Party. Deloria argues, "like the revolutionary who was both shoemaker and Indian chief, hobbyists were simultaneously nonconformists and people who worked doubly hard to comply with two cultural codes. As Indians, they were not only members of two well-defined communities, but also unique, self-directed individuals--confident actors in an organic world of tradition and successful denizens of modernity. These dual identities were possible because hobbyists imagined Indian Others as authentic, yet accessible—culturally close and racially distant" (147).

I met David and the other Indians at the North Park site the weekend after Pioneer Days; it was my day off from working at the museum. One of the female re-enactors took me to a public bathroom to help me get dressed. I belted a thick wool blanket around my hips, and hooked wool leggings over my calves. I pulled a dingy linen tunic over my head, and took off my watch and earrings. This was serious play. Nothing modern. I parted my hair in the center and wrapped my ponytail with red silk ribbon. When I came out, David inspected me. He dipped a finger in red grease paint and ran it along the part in my hair and the tops of my ears, and then dotted my cheeks. The camp nodded their approval.

I sat with my legs folded and angled to one side, the way I was told to do. Someone gave me a turkey-wing fan to hold.

"You need a story," said Tom, another re-enactor. I was bewildered. He looked at me for a moment, thinking. "You're my little sister. You're a Shawnee."

I should mention that my skin is terrifically pale. My hair is reddish; my eyes are gray-blue. I don't look like a "real" Indian, the way Deloria and others have defined the word—that simulation, that construction. And so I became a white captive. How captive? It was up to me. Tom helped me to create a story in which my parents were slain by a passing war party, and I was taken as an infant to be the replacement for his lost sister. I would never remember being white. I had my clothing and makeup, as correct as could be determined. I had my story. I even had a name, Little Sister. I was an Indian. I was history.

In the aftermath of World War II, Americans were looking to define or redefine their identities. Deloria comments that for white Americans, many of whom took refuge in newly-constructed and racially homogeneous suburbs, "many postwar constructions of ethnic and racial Others emphasized close, interior qualities that encouraged white appropriation and self-discovery" (141). Suddenly lacking glamorous and meaningful methods of self-definition, many whites chose to identify with the constructed Other. Deloria claims that "a range of ideas suggested that social boundary crossing was primarily a question of behavior. Anthropology provided a model for such transgression. Music, dance, and literature afforded personal paths of entry into other cultures. In the postwar United States, these notions transcended the hobby, as American constructed a variety of extraordinarily accessible Others" (141). After World War II, it was easier than ever before for whites to play Indian.

The French and Indian War started in 1754 and lasted for nine years, even though it was part of the transatlantic

Seven Years War. Considering the enormity and complexity of the task that it enabled—the authorship of America, down to its dominant language—the French and Indian War receives little attention in children's history books. It's always overshadowed by the American Revolution, and swallowed by the national pride that compels the telling and retelling of that tale. That summer, the Fort Pitt Museum had a project: to re-imagine the museum itself, and to begin preparations for a major renovation. My employers were interested in promoting the museum as a pivotal node for two upcoming national events and their massive marketing campaigns. The first was the 200th anniversary of the Lewis & Clark Expedition, a valorous event in the history of America, which the Lewis & Clark Bicentennial Council would "re-create" with festivals and tourism. The second event was the 250th anniversary of the French and Indian War, the war my employers—and the re-enactors—were interested in renaming "The War for Empire."

The War for Empire. Imperialism is a dirty word; it's considered antithetical to the very idea of America. But for America to exist, there had to be an empire. It's what America first defined itself against. America broke away from the empire of the British. But then, America purchased a quarter of itself from the empire of France. America wrested the remainder of itself from the empire of Spain and the republic of Texas and the nation of Mexico. America headed north and south to find the rest of itself in on the land that held Alaska and Hawaii. And Puerto Rico. And Guam. And the Virgin Islands, American Samoa, the Northern Mariana Islands. And the Philippines, for a time. And Guantanamo Bay, of course. These are all the pieces of the body of America. America found its body parts, all of its stories, using one powerful story, the doctrine of Manifest Destiny. While the doctrine itself may have fallen out of polite speech in America, it inhabits the stories that make up America.

In the museum gift shop, I bought a kit for making a cornhusk doll so I would have something to do while I was sitting around the fair. I pulled the pre-cut corn husks from their plastic wrapper, soaked them in water, and cut and tied them into a rough human shape. A bit of horsetail was included in the kit to make hair; the instructions dictated that I was to make two braids and secure them onto the doll's head with a strip of husk for a headband. This was not what my hair, or the hair of any of the women around me, looked like. Instead, I found find a way to make a single ponytail at the back of the head. I made a male doll, too, with a darker bit of husk for a breech-cloth. I gave them to the children of re-enactors, whose parents had dragged them to this elaborate game of dress-up. As I worked, I wondered if the 18th century natives in this part of the world had ever made corn-husk dolls. Did they make dolls at all, the way I would think of a doll? What were dolls to them, and what are they to me? What were these dolls to the public, these suburbanites watching me? Was the doll simply something I could do, something I could make to prove to the audience I was authentic? Curious and rustic handicrafts. Someone else's idea of a doll, someone else's idea of an Indian, neither one human.

In speaking of the atrocities caused by Manifest Destiny, Vizenor states that these histories "are now the simulations of dominance, and the causes of the conditions that have become manifest manners in literature . . . The simulations of manifest manners are the continuation of the surveillance and domination of the tribes in literature. Simulations are the absence of the tribal real" (5). What is the right way for my body to tell a story? Perhaps I should ask, what is the right story for my body to tell? Is it a story made of cornhusk dolls in plastic packages? If it were quillwork, or rush-mats that I knew how to make, would anything be different?

112

"How," the people said. Hello, *the girl replied.*

"You don't look like an Indian," the people said. I am Shawnee, *the girl replied.*

"Who are you?" the people asked. The girl stood up and spoke. She told a story about a little white girl found in the woods, about a brother who needed a sister. A story about a husband at war, and a daughter dying of smallpox. The people listened and walked away, and more people came to see the girl. She told the story, always the same story, over and over. Know your story.

What story?

Once I had been doing the festival circuit for a while as a re-enactor, I was invited to speak at an elementary school. It was me, fur trader Bob, and warrior David. We set up the conical lodge behind the school, and I seated myself out-side of it. The two men went to their stations, and a class of young children arrived for the show. "Here is the Indian princess in her tee-pee," their plump, middle-aged teacher said loudly as she directed the students to me. "Come on, don't you want to see the Indian princess?" I bristled at her words, even though by then I had gotten used to gently "cor-recting" the public. "I am not a princess," I said. "And this is not a tipi. I don't know that word. This is a conical lodge." The teacher didn't bat an eyelash; her smile was large and white. And so I told my story again, about my husband who had to fight, about my daughter who was dying of smallpox. I was nervous, but I tried to make as much eye contact as I could.

A tall boy wrinkled his nose at me. "Where'd you get those hair barrettes?"

"From the traders," I stammered, caught off guard. I hadn't hid my bobby pins well enough. The boy looked un-convinced. "Come on, we need to go see the Indian chief now," said the teacher. The children said their goodbyes and walked away, but one girl ran back and threw her arms around me. "I hope your daughter gets better," she said.

Know your story.

Whose story?

Vizenor writes, "Manifest manners are the simulations of bourgeois decadence and melancholy" (11).

And, "This portrait is not an Indian" (44).

I have to ask myself why I chose to re-enact. I was not a historian then and I am not a historian now. It wasn't part of my job description. I was at the museum from 8 to 5, Monday through Friday, filing papers, taking inventory of artifacts, straightening the shelves of canon replicas in the gift shop, and reading more about the war so I could assist the public if they came in. But now, I am reconsidering what I have been taught about what it means to be a writer, and what writing should be for. And yes, I find I am thinking about history, and what histories I carry in my body. What are the histories I have tried to carry in my body, the histories I have tried to be a surrogate for? What representations, what simulations I have tried to carry into the world, and for what reasons?

Simulations. In speaking more about these, Vizenor invokes Baudrillard:

The simulations of manifest manners are treacherous and elusive in histories; how ironic that the most secure simulations are unreal sensations, and become the real without a referent to an actual tribal remembrance. Tribal realities are superseded by simulations of the unreal, and tribal wisdom is weakened by those imitations, however sincere. The pleasure of silence, natural reason, the rights of consciousness, transformation of the marvelous, and the pleasure of trickster stories are misconstrued in the simulations of dominance; manifest manners are the absence of the real in the ruins of tribal representations. (8)

114

I'm coming to understand that this time of re-enacting was not the first time I played Indian. When I was about tem, my favorite book was Scott O'Dell's *Island of the Blue Dolphins*, the story of an indigenous American woman stranded alone on an island for twenty years. I also loved Jean Craighead George's *Julie of the Wolves*, about a young Inuit girl—again stranded, alone—trying to find her father. I spent hours in my backyard constructing makeshift spears and bows and arrows out of felled tree branches, pieces of slate from the yard, and yarn from my own stash of craft supplies. I acted the story out, changed it, made it into my own story. For a long time I looked back on those days as wildly innocent and romantic, formative of my personality as a loner, a non-conformist of some sort, and of my desire to be a writer, or some kind of maker of things. In some ways, it was a time before I clearly saw the darkness in my own manners, the outlines I drew around the Other. Most likely, it was a time when the Other and I were friends because I could make the Other play innocent, play my game of Indian with me, imaginary empire in my head, carried in my hands.

Vizenor says, "the simulations of dominance and absence of the other are the concern of manifest manners." (12).

"You don't look like an Indian."
 I am Shawnee.
 "Don't you miss your real *family?"*
 I don't remember.
 "Wouldn't you rather be with your people?"
 I am happy.

I used to wonder why they called my city the city of three rivers. The rivers that ran around the park could just as soon be the Mississippi, or the St. Lawrence. Aren't they all the same river? I asked when I was a child. In my mind, there was no way to divide the waters except with land, marking

115

them as fine and discrete. Even now I wonder if the three rivers are more than what they are in the minds of those who live around them. Will they always be what they are? I know that they will cut several thousand more feet until they hit bedrock, leaving the Point a high and beaten peninsula. Or, the rivers will swallow the peninsula, leaving only traces of what's underneath. They've done this before. Inside the museum, a sign mounted three feet off of the ground on a support column says "High Water Mark—Flood of '97." The museum lost a good many artifacts; displays were ruined, books swollen, the print washed out. The museum closed for many months. In that time, it ceased to exist as a museum— it was only another casualty of the floodwaters that pressed on beyond the Point, onto the Mon Wharf, across the streets of the city. The river owned the city then. It will own the city again someday, I could be assured.

Who owns the French and Indian War? Not the re-enactors. Not the descendants of its fighters, whoever they might be. Not a group of museum administrators in Harrisburg. Vizenor writes about the individuals he calls "postindian warriors," those who "encounter their enemies with the same courage in literature as their ancestors once evinced on horses, and they create their stories with a new sense of survivance. The warriors bear the simulations of their time and counter the manifest manners of domination" (4). Despite my insistence on trying to be an ally, wasn't I, by virtue of my position, absent from any just and intimate negotiation of postindian survivance? I "played" a Shawnee of the 18th century, on some of the earliest-marked land for battle. I was trying, in earnest, to be authentic, to resist by existence. I was trying to be a person, a person with a story. But my story was written and told through a filter. It was told from underneath blankets dyed by white housewives. From underneath paint mass-produced in China. From behind turkey feathers purchased with a MasterCard. Simulations. And me,

116

a white girl, a simulation of other whites, a simulation of a white story of an Indian, white creation.

Vizenor says: "Manifest manners and the simulations of dominance are the annihilation, not the survivance of tribal stories" (9).

One of the last re-enactments I did was the Haunted History Hayride, which takes place in late October at Bushy Run Battlefield, another French & Indian War site about 40 miles east of the Fort Pitt museum. The small group of cabins, barns, and pavilions that made up Bushy Run were on vast acres of land with no city shadowing them. In the bathroom of the site's tiny gift shop, I donned my dress and jewelry and styled my hair as usual, but I added a layer of pale makeup to my already-pale face, and ran black grease paint under and around my eyes. I dotted my face and neck with red. On the Haunted History Hayride, I was one of the Indians at the smallpox camp.

The smallpox camp was five white females dressed as Indians, faces decorated with thick, clumsy simulations of what we thought smallpox might have looked like. We sat under a conical lodge, clutching heavy wool blankets around us. It was bitter cold, and no light save for that from a small campfire we struggled to keep burning. We rehearsed our scene: when the cart arrived, we would allow the public to look at us as we enacted the death of a small crying child— played by the daughter of one of the other re-enactors. Beth, a middle-school French teacher, taught us a few words to say. Every time a cart arrived, two of us would approach it still shouldering our blankets, calling out in French. "Madame, Monsieur, s'il vous plaît."

Vizenor asserts:

The tribes bear the simulation of pathos and the tragic without the wisdom of chance and natural miseries of the seasons. Simulation of the tragic has been sustained by the literature of dominance. Natural reason teases the sense that nature is precarious; however, the realities of chance, fate, and tragic wisdom were denied in the literature of dominance. (15)

Is this the right story?

I got more and more insistent with each pass of the cart, tugging on clothing, staring directly into children's faces: "Mademoiselle, mon Dieu, s'il vous plaît!" I was suddenly furious. I wanted to desperately to scare a little girl or boy so deeply that he or she would know what happened there.

What really happened.

But did *I* know what really happened?

And were the people on the carts just playing with me? They played at being horrified, while I played at being wounded, diseased, tragic, angry? And when we parted, would both of us go back and play at being outraged, would we both play the game of rationalization, satisfaction, the quiet, mannered game of contemporary America?

Why can't I let it go, wash it from my life like it never happened? And why do I keep thinking about it? Is it because I am still this girl who played Indian, a child, a child-woman who cannot stop with her games? Maybe it's repetition compulsion, neurosis driving me to recreate the acts again and again without remembering and coming to terms with their source. Or maybe the whole practice of playing Indian is repeating without remembering. But I am still the day someone declared my mother's family farm to be along "Moccasin Hollow Road." I am in the arrowheads my uncles pulled out of their plowed farmland and put on display in the house, and passed on to me. I am in the high-school mascots of the white suburbanites—the Warriors and the Vikings. The oldest evidence of contact in this land. Vikings. Warriors. Natives. Indians. Lacan says that "we cannot confine ourselves to giving a new truth its rightful place, for the point is to take up our place in it. The truth requires us to go out of our way. We cannot do so by simply getting used to it. We get used to reality. The truth we repress" (433). I often forget that I am white, but when I remember, I remember that that forgetfulness is the privilege of whiteness. I frequently forget that I am American, but when I remember, I remember that that forgetfulness is the privilege of Americanness. And I remember Malea Powell saying, *"there's so much more involved in being able to have this story than the telling of it can hold. The having spills over, the seemingly unutterable excess of the story"* (14).

Maybe all I can do is expose my own racism, my own acts of domination and appropriation, to a critical light, neither harsh nor sympathetic. Measure and re-measure my intentions against the weight of my body on this land. This time it was only a fragment, a tiny piece of myself that I managed to free. But I watched it curl up and burn from the inside out, the ashes falling like words, falling between earth and flesh into the story of the world.

Works Cited

Deloria, Philip J. *Playing Indian*. New Haven: Yale UP, 1998.

Freud, Sigmund. *Beyond the Pleasure Principle*. NY: Liverpool P, 1961.

Lacan, Jacques. "The Instance of the Letter in the Unconscious." *Ecrits: The First Complete Edition in English*. Bruce Fink, trans. NY: Norton, 2006.

Lyons, Scott Richard. "Rhetorical Sovereignty: What Do American Indians Want from Writing?" *College Composition and Communication* 51 (Feb 2000): 447–68.

Powell, Malea. "Listening to Ghosts." *Alt Dis: Alternative Discourses and the Academy*. Eds. Christopher Schroeder, Helen Fox, and Patricia Bizzell. Portsmouth: Boynton/Cook, 2002. 11–22.

Vizenor, Gerald. *Manifest Manners: Postindian Warriors of Survivance*. Hanover: UP of New England, 1994.

Jami Frush

Dear Refugee

Dear refugee,

I've had my ear to the wall. Trying to hear your voice through the cracks in the paint. It's been hard though. The color of my wall is Cotton Cream. I imagine you. I don't know who does the naming.

I heard about you on the news. I thought you were a "special humanitarian concern" and should be allowed to nest, to roam free. Migratory birds are expected to return.

When the dust on my floor came together in a ball of hot mess, I thought of the dance of tumbleweeds. They are specific to dry locations. The way blue birds belong.

Can I tell you? The texture of the walls is a combination of smooth and gritty. I imagine you making your lover coffee every morning, like something of the Earth, sand.

I had my ear to the wall. Trying to find the center of it. A feather from my blanket dropped to the floor. This is lonely. Where are you?

Maybe you were at your wooden desk once, licking envelopes. Maybe she calls to you from another room telling you that your soup is warm-blooded and your eggs are ready. Maybe my imagination blurs the whole thing.

I have my ear to a cup to a wall to your story.

Sarah Wynn

There Must Have Been Two

To see the rusted license plate, the bumper
falling off you have to leave the road.
There are trees grown up between
the gravel pathway and here (houses all
around, but you wouldn't know).

There are no dents from before, only
from the branches, the animal claws,
and the wind of Oklahoma. No prior damage
means no prior accident, but I still
can't imagine that it was left in anything
but a rush.

And I wonder about the driver's door—
closed—how he must have calmly shut his side
as his passenger left quickly, rose up
and clicked her own door open, left
it swinging in the wind and the dust,
the same dust that would carry her
onward, past the forest, to the gravel
and the concrete, and further on still
to the bridge over red murky
lakes, into some town that she
had been searching for all along.

MARK WISNIEWSKI

Used

even back then that '63 Falcon
was uncommonly old
& thus ill-equipped
for collision & as I rose on a curve
merging from one freeway
to another to visit
a woman who preferred drink
to me it all at once died

leaving me
motionless
Texans in traffic threatening to appear
in my rear-view with no time to stop
themselves from killing me

I dropped the transmission
to neutral rolled backward
only as fast
as the curved downgrade allowed: my
one sane out

in this manner I made it from the right
lane onto the left &

then still
left onto the emergency lane

where I sat in park absorbing
the afterglow of risk

CHAD WOODY

Johnnie Two Crows

Five winters ago, my old friend Johnnie "Two Crows" Wenger was hit by a truck. That was the beginning of his transformation: into a bullshit artist, a shyster, an imitation Indian, and a man who is no longer my friend. This is hard to admit, because everybody else treats him like a hero, and he did pull off an amazing feat of recovery. He also managed to do something most people never do. He changed. I mean really changed, in his nature. Maybe it was like the famous story from medical history, when Phineas Gage got a railroad spike blasted through his brain and survived as a much angrier man—a change in the body forcing a change in the man. But with Johnnie, the change didn't happen right after the accident. First I thought he was broken and ready to accept defeat. He would just sprout from a wheelchair for the rest of his life and forget the rest, maybe stay with friends and do their taxes or something to make himself useful. Settle into a porch full of herb gardening under the chubby gaze of an assisted-living nurse. That's what the old Johnnie would have done.

Instead, he landed in a crumbling old farmhouse out on the edge of the Creek nation. This alone was a license to fester and decline. It was the house his parents died in, and it looked like he might, too. Deep in the soil of his concussed brain, though, he was regrowing himself as if from a different seed. His parents' house would be his Bat-Cave, his metamorphosis cocoon. I was one of several people who went to visit him there. It was not a showcase for reasons to live. For starters, it needed work. It was like a Grant Wood painting turning into a source for raw barnwood. There were birds and squirrels living in the attic, constantly scratching around above the bedrooms. When it rained, it leaked around the chimney, and directly in the middle of the kitchen, which had ceiling stains growing into three-dimensional plasterboard warts like inverted volcanoes or stubby stalactites. From the windows you could see some nice trees, a weedy meadow, and in the distance, the parking lot of a casino. One window was broken, and when I looked through I had to turn away after imagining heaving myself from a wheelchair neck-first into the gashing knives of glass rimming the opening. Before I left the room, I pulled the hostile shards from their plastery slots and tossed them out into the grass.

Like everybody and his brother around here, Johnny claimed some fraction of Indian blood in him. Most of the people who even bring it up are just scamming somebody—maybe only themselves, to feel more like the underdog, more "in tune" with the earth, or somehow just less culpable in the bastard canvas around them. Everybody wants to be an outsider, at least since rock-n-roll. But a few blood cells don't change anything, in my book. Being a sixteenth Chickasaw ("Hickasaw," some joke, because of long-standing entanglements in redneck family trees) won't really change the way you laugh at *Cheers* or the way you gulp Gatorade, but it might get you a free ride to Oklahoma State, or at least your books paid for. Or it might plant a seed of delusion.

Johnnie wobbled around that house for half a year before the right ingredients fell into the stew of his mind. I think some variation of the phrase "You'll probably never walk again" echoed off the walls of his skull as he read some weird comic books and who knows what else, maybe some conspiracy talk radio, or just his own crazy ideas. The one thing I know he did hear was a pair of crows always squawking around outside his house, because that's where he got

the name "Two Crows." His year of recuperating was punc-
tuated by their cries. He decided they were talking to him,
becoming his totem animals, telling him about some great
destiny. He thought of them as spirit guides, and maybe his
parents' ghosts. He never said this to me, but he implied it
once. I think he was desperately fucking nuts and ready to
believe anything. At the time I thought, "whatever gets you
through the day without blowing your brains out, buddy."
That place would have driven me crazy, too.

Here's the big idea that evolved from Johnnie's primitive
ooze of a scenario: he would recover his body by "dying,"
then coming back up the evolutionary ladder, using Native
American animal totems as footholds. Supposedly dragging
his astral body or his spirit or whatever up through different
primal forms would teach his legs to work again. The whole
thing would start with a controlled blackout, he said.

"What, like those guys who die choking themselves for
an orgasm?" I said.

"No. Well, same basic thing, but this isn't sexual. I'm
accessing my reptilian brain," Johnnie said without a trace
of humor. "Pure survival mode. Reptiles can regrow major
body parts."

"Well, yeah, but WE can't. Sorry, but if you're looking
for somebody to choke you until you pass out, ask someone
else. Too creepy, plus, you're on a shitload of pain killers.
What if you just die?"

"I'm cutting the pain killers down," he said, and that was
it. He knew I wasn't on board, so he didn't tell me any more,
but if he had, it might have gone something like:

"I'm not going to ask anyone to choke me. I'm going to
asphyxiate myself, and someone else will save me."

And I would have said, "Shit, that sounds like a BAD
IDEA. Don't be a suicidal idiot."

Far as I know, Johnnie just planned his little death for one of his Monday-Wednesday-Friday in-home care visits. He hung a pair of wire-cutters on the door handle, with a little note that said, "help." When the nurse came in, there he was slumped onto the floor with a zip-tie tight around his neck and everything above it raging purple. It was easy for her to clip the zip-tie off, and then she slapped him awake. I don't think he really died, but I guess it was close enough. He was on his primordial way. The nurse quit after that, but not before she relieved her car of all the epsom salt he'd asked her to buy. She had to clean out two local stores to get 20 cartons. Johnnie said he needed to soak his legs a lot. Not a lie, technically.

The next step was his homemade primordial soup. A week-long soak in salty bathwater in a pitch-black bathroom. Sensory deprivation to cut away his human sensory apparatus and become amoebalike, and let's hope he was getting out to use the toilet.

Johnnie also had his friend Go-Dog helping him. I don't know what this guy's real name is, but it doesn't matter: he's a dumbass pothead, but I'm sure he looks at it more like being one of our local experts on touring other dimensions pharmaceutically. Go-Dog was stealing berries from the Creek nation land nearby and feeding them to Johnnie, who told him where to look. I'm sure they had some big ideas about the healing energy of native berries, not to mention whatever weed Go-Dog was growing back there. A good way to get away with anything is to do it on someone else's land.

I could picture Johnnie crawling out of the primordial soup, dripping saltwater and holding the windowsill, shaking to hold the weight of his torso off his failed vertebrae, finding that, yes, he could stand for a moment, turning toward a towel but clenching as invisible pliers took hold of some nerve in his spine, lowering himself slowly onto the edge of the tub. I could picture Go-Dog bent and running with a butter tub full of blackberries, from the tall grass of the Creek nation to the cover of the round bales left behind by Johnnie's dad, two hundred feet of stone-gray humps becoming moldy soil after five years in the weather. I could picture whatever I wanted, but that doesn't mean it happened that way.

A few months after Johnnie's controlled suicide thing, I stopped by his house after work one day. The leaves were just off the trees and it was getting dark early now—just behind his house, an orangey sunset bled out. The house looked haunted, black curtainless windows reflecting dim sky. His old pickup sat by the barn, so I assumed he was home, but no one came to the door. I knocked harder, then walked around back, damp leaves clumping around my shoes. Near the back door, behind a crumbling stack of firewood, I finally saw light in a window—just a glint, like a candle. I banged on the door. "Hey Johnnie!" A minute later he approached, clunking along. Sounded like his wheelchair was broken. But when the door opened, there he was, standing.

"Hey, Tim," he said, leaning on a thick wooden cane.

"Holy shit, man, you're up? I can't believe you're walking already!"

"Yeah, for like two weeks now." He seemed quiet, distant, and slightly uncomfortable. The standing was probably a strain.

"I just wanted to see if you needed anything, if you want my help painting the house next year, or maybe this fall if we get an Indian summer. I guess we won't have to bother pouring those wheelchair ramps." I'd come onto the doorstep without even realizing the plywood ramp was already gone.

"I'm good. Thanks for coming by. Don't really need anything."

"Can I come in? Is this place still the same?"

"Uh, pretty much. Not much to see."

"Yeah, 'cause it's so dark," I said, flipping the switch right by the door. No light came on.

"The power's off. I didn't pay the bill."

"Aw, shit . . . do you need some money, or . . . ?"

"Oh, no, I've got money. I just didn't pay it. On purpose."

"Why? You turning Amish now?" My eyes were adjusting to the muddy interior, and I could see a little of the living room. There was a big pile of little cardboard boxes in there.

"No, but that might not be a bad idea," Johnnie said as if weighing his options. He finally leaned away, wincing and mincing back to what he'd been doing. There were two candles burning in the large room he entered, but I hesitated to call it a living room anymore. All his folks' stuff was gone, and I mean ALL of it, except for a wooden chair, and this appeared to be house-wide. In the middle of the room was a three-foot-tall pyramid made of, not little boxes, but bricks. On the opposite wall, crude drawings of animals, almost like cave paintings, on a rising diagonal. At the bottom was a watery blob, then an arrow, a fish, another arrow . . . on up to a little human outline that reminded me of the people on the Olympic medals they gave out a few Olympics ago in Norway.

"So… you've been a fish, a snake, a lizard, a bird, a mouse, a bear, a caveman, and now you're like, an Egyptian," I said, nodding at the pyramid. "Oh, and a blob at the beginning," I smiled. I was relieved when he actually cracked a slight smile.

"Yeah. The blob was probably the hardest one," he sighed. "You'd think it would be easy. Amoeba is what I was after. And this is more like a Mayan pyramid—you know, a ziggurat."

"Oh yeah, more the Native American version," I said, trying not to sound dismissive. I just didn't know how jokey I could be about any of this. We used to make fun of anything and everything, but the guy was developing some sort of redneck mysticism that resisted jokes. Johnnie was looking out the window. Lining the windowsill was a row of jars and jugs filled with amber liquid. I was about to say something about him being addicted to apple juice when I made the connection: piss jugs. No electricity meant no well water, no flushing toilet. Kind of an eerie light came through those jars, like dark honey or preservative goo for body parts in a Frankenstein movie.

"So," I said, "you probably don't want one of those new digital TVs for Christmas, huh?" He looked at me blankly for two seconds, then said, "I don't think I'll be doing Christmas anymore."

"That's OK, man," I said, smiling. "You know I wasn't getting you jack shit for Christmas anyway." That's the sort of casual bastardism we used to toss off all the time, but this time it had an undercurrent of seriousness, like a parting of ways.

On the way out I told him again to call me if he needed anything. What I wanted to say was, "You're nuts, bucko," but there he stood with all the evidence: he was walking around, living the miracle, and that's the thing about beliefs—as long as you're winning, you can believe whatever the hell you want. It's when you start losing big that your system collapses.

After all this weird shit with Johnnie in his den of totems, his telling me that he wasn't doing Christmas anymore is what stuck in my craw, mentally. I'm not even some great champion of Christmas; I don't care if you write "X-Mas" or even if you slap a "Fuck Santa" bumper sticker on your car, but it's a basic American tradition to take a break in the dead of winter, eat a lot, maybe bake some cookies with your mom, buy people crap they don't need and pretend you did it all for Jesus. The fact is, even Wal-Mart closes for Christmas. I wanted to send Johnnie a note that said, "You are not bigger than Wal-Mart—get ready for Christmas, motherfucker." I guess it was proof of how much he was getting to me. I was daydreaming about sending abusive mail to a guy recovering from a crushed spine. He didn't even have any family to celebrate Christmas with, which might be the reason he was skipping it. Little did I know that it could have been the first clue about his new girlfriend.

A season passed with nothing between Johnnie and me, and I believe I developed a mistaken view of his life. Of course I wondered what came after the pyramid in his symbolic scheme to whittle himself out of every branch of the animal kingdom, but what I really wondered was how he endured the view from his dilapidated purgatory. His parents had both died young, seemingly stamping an early expiration date on their son. He'd just had a strong preview of his own mortality, and now he had no furniture, no more in-home care, and no one but Go-Dog to impress. I imagined him home alone and semi-hopeless, drinking discount beer while staring at a brick pyramid all day, taking painful walks into the woods to pour out his piss jugs and maybe watch his reincarnated parents fight over an acorn or a dead mouse or whatever crows eat. I imagined him alone, but that's where I was wrong.

No, sir. Johnnie was making friends and getting pussy. This news first broke from the mouth of Go-Dog when I ran into him at a gas station—not exactly Walter Cronkite, but it wasn't long before most of his pot-scented lore was shown to be true.

Johnnie had fallen under the spell of Bathsheba Brandt, eldest daughter of Jed Brandt, owner of the biggest local employer of grunt labor, Area's Best Roofing, and godfather of the biggest local cult, the Jehovah's Witnesses. Bathsheba and her sister Melody drove around town in a big white Ford pickup with decal lettering on the windshield that said "JEHOVAH," alternately running errands for their dad and for the almighty (My uncle liked using that label as their name, as in, "I drove by Jehovah's place today…"). Jed was basically a good old guy, if basically clueless, but his daughters were slightly different shades of awful. Go-Dog said Bathsheba and Melody stopped at Johnnie's place in the Jehovah Truck one day, spreading The Word, and sniffed out Johnnie's poverty. Bathsheba gave him money for gas, loaded him down with Watchtower magazines (if you can call those scrawny little pamphlets *magazines*), and insisted he come to church, which he did later that very day.

Apparently Go-Dog dropped in on Johnnie one day, probably trying to sell a baggie or two of pot, and found Bathsheba there acting like the lady of the house. The power was back on and she was making French toast with like a whole can of cherry pie filling dumped over two pieces of toast, served with rinsed-out beer bottles full of milk.

Bathsheba was a strange creature, but I can't say I blamed Johnnie for getting involved with her. She was far from hideous, with energy that one might call "spunk" if that didn't bring to mind independent girls not beholden to a throwback religion demanding obedience to God and one's father. She had this frizzled amber hair and wide eyes as if her nerves were amped up too high, zapping 220 volts through 110 wiring. Her frumpy dress, intended to minimize sexuality, could be seen as an odd turn-on: the long skirts and tucked blouses she and Melody wore were unusual in this age of t-shirts and tight jeans, and both women had outstanding shelf-butts, as in you could damn near set a wine glass atop their ass and send it to the next table. Ironically, this woman who did not wear pants was probably wearing the proverbial pants, steering Johnnie around as if he were still wheelchair-bound.

I chuckled when I realized I had the next piece of the evolutionary puzzle: Who wiped out and replaced the American Indians? The Christians, especially the pushy ones.

I probably shouldn't say Johnnie was "getting pussy." Honestly, who knows? For all I know, Bathsheba just adopted him as a special project—someone who obviously needed a helping hand, who also might be ripe for spiritual conversion. Even from the sexless Jehovah's Witnesses, sex was the easiest thing to imagine, but even if they were fooling around, there's only so many minutes a day that's likely to eat up. Maybe they were just canning pickled beets or making caramel apples in the kitchen of the Kingdom Hall or something. Well, the caramel apples might be considered too sinful and Halloweenish, too risky to make in the church facilities. They might as well just hump in the pews.

Admittedly, I judged Bathsheba unfairly by association with her sister Melody, who had been one of our classmates in high school. She was a busty, disagreeable slut—pretty in some contaminated way, with beautiful long dark hair, but somehow she was bitch enough to sour a sunny day. I always found Melody to be a vile person, and pure she was not. She fucked at least a half-dozen guys in high school, threatening to expose a couple of them as rapists if any adults found out, but she acted like she wore a golden chastity belt. Bathsheba had more of an eccentric reputation (not quite up to the nickname "Batshit," that I'd heard a few times), but where Melody was concerned, I'd always held that maybe you'd rather stick your dick in a fistful of centipedes.

As if to demonstrate the mining process for a weird mix of beliefs, Johnnie was also going to what I call "Indian Church." On weekends, a big group of locals—tribespeople and their friends—gathered at a ramshackle pavilion on the reservation and played games, sang songs, traded crafts, and shared stories. This was exactly the sort of thing you might see on the news where tribal elders sometimes don their headdresses and do rain dances or whatever. Indian Church was where Go-Dog caught up with Johnnie, and it was also apparently a crackpot smorgasbord. Saturdays they held a swap meet of sorts. If you wanted a dream catcher or some junk turquoise jewelry or little baggies of peyote buttons or some magical half-coyote puppies with luck powers, Indian Church was where you wanted to be. Plus, as long as you kept them hidden when you drove back into town, even il-legal drugs were legal there, or at least tolerated by "the white man." Go-Dog rarely missed a lick of Indian Church.

Lives like ours prove the inescapable sadness equations of small towns: Johnnie's truck sagging in the same muddy ruts it had been carving since high school, my van tracing the same daily paths as I ran service calls around the county for the only electrical contractor in town, the same crews of old guys yapping in the same diner chairs eating the same pies baked by the same old ladies . . . everyone knows everybody, and we watch each other fly or fall, but always confined to this little box of a place. So few of us get out, and the ones who do just leave the tribe smaller and weaker, because the ones who leave are the ones with guts, or maybe just the most terror of staying.

Even Johnnie and Bathsheba, seen as a fresh new couple, were like brother and sister in a way: only two years apart in the same school our whole lives, siblings riding the same buses and playing on the same teams, hating the same rival quarterbacks and cheerleaders.

Only a few months of Bathsheba's home cooking had Johnnie off his cane and walking like a new man. I saw him in town maybe once a month, and I swear you'd never guess he'd been sold a wheelchair for a paraplegic two years ear-lier. I'm sure his doctor was embarrassed to show his face in our town. My old friend was jogging, working, and praying to some weird mix of Christian and new age beliefs. That's when the real craziness began.

Johnnie took up kickboxing, in addition to forming a sort of health cult. It all started at Indian Church. There you could find a small group of ex-military guys, Vietnam to Desert Storm, who were into sparring and survivalism. As you might expect, they came from lots of Creek blood—joining the service was the quickest way off the reservation for young guys—and they preached that nutty peaceful warrior stuff that made you think, "This guy could maybe wig out and beat me to death with a sock full of crystals." I knew one of them, Quentin Tate, from rewiring his house, and he was nothing but helpful and upstanding. You just might not want to shake him awake abruptly in the dark, or burn his house down with a bad wiring mistake.

At the same time, Johnnie's farm was becoming headquarters for the aggressively kooky. Johnnie had visited the crackpot smorgasbord enough that he was emerging as one of its "head chefs." A new sign by his driveway read "The Healthy Millennium Farm." Lots of people were visiting, leasing little plots for organic farming, listening to Johnnie talk about his miraculous recovery, and learning that it was all due to the healing properties of water, which apparently had a form of memory in Johnnie's world. Water was God's living appendage, eroding mountains, sustaining grasslands, and transforming our bodies if we knew how to channel the current. Water bound the world together, and its molecules retained some knowledge of all it touched, imprinted like liquid circuitry (that's my own comparison, and I admit it comes packaged with an image of the mercury-like T-1000 Terminator). I think it was all related to homeopathic medicine. It finally occurred to me that those piss jugs I saw might have been more than just substitutes for plumbing—diluted urine was apparently considered medicine on the Healthy Millennium Farm.

I couldn't bear to go there myself or even ask the man himself about it, but I had my friends-of-friends sources (one of Johnnie's acolytes was the talkative nephew of our electric company secretary). Basically, the higher the bullshit quotient went, the more people ate that shit up. Having his

134

own snake-oil farm had made Johnny a full-blown leper messiah. He was taking desperate old folks and cancer victims to "water vortexes," handing out rules for water drinking, and campaigning against vaccines, not to mention some kind of talk about synchronicity and time being "cubed," so that people live three days for every perceived day, whatever the fuck that means. I was just waiting for the trepanning to begin.

Whichever hybrid martial art they were practicing led to a Creek Area ToughMan Tournament, which Johnnie surely had to compete in to prove his vitality. I decided to go and watch, dreading the outcome. The event was headlined by two more famous fighters whose names seemed to rephrase, unofficially, White man vs. Indian. Most of the audience, however, was made up of locals there to see Johnnie Two Crows, our area's greatest medicine man.

If we made the Hollywood movie about Johnnie, he'd have to get kicked in the spine and re-paralyzed at this point, with only his faith and his devoted wife to save him. But that's not what happened. He won his fight even though he was more beat up than the other guy, and they both had to spend thousands of dollars in the ER to make sure they didn't have concussions. Johnnie's injuries were not major, but his woman did not seem amused. His prize was only $500, which didn't even cover the cost of the ambulance, much less the CAT scan, so he was in the hole. That is, until his magic water cult doubled in size in the following weeks.

Bathsheba must have gotten pregnant around that time, though I wouldn't know that until much later. They weren't married, and were officially living in sin, which I assume was a big problem with her family, possibly an unbridgable rift. She was no longer seen driving the JEHOVAH truck, now piloted by her evil sister. The Brandt family was out of the picture, at least until regret or grandparental instincts kicked in. Bathsheba and Johnnie were riding high, writing their own future, but finally all that mattered from this time was that Bathsheba was under no medical supervision for her pregnancy.

The last time I saw Johnnie was the last anyone around here saw of him. As soon as I heard that his baby was born dead, I drove to his place, parking on the road near the closed gate. Bathsheba was said to be recovering in the hospital after extensive bleeding and mental distress.

After all that had happened, there I was again with Johnnie in his parents' dark house, looking at the wall of animal totems—sigils, he'd called them. I studied them, too, as if helping him search for some new answer. This time the room was furnished with all the usual feminine touches, everything just so, except for the haunted man sitting on the floor and the large section of wallpaper peeled back in front of him. This time I didn't turn the light switch on, and neither of us said anything for long moments.

In raw and hopeless musings he told me things I knew and things I never dreamed. He said his wife almost died and still might die. I didn't even know they were married. He said his baby was born briefly gasping, but it was meant to breathe water, it had gills and looked like a bloody salamander, it came too soon, not human yet.

He said he skipped the amphibian stage—look at the wall.

He said he saved water from the amniotic sac, just a drop but that was enough.

He said he couldn't find his parents.

He said he must have been wrong about some things, but nothing had changed, he knew the way.

He said *please leave*.

That night Johnnie's house burned to the foundation and he disappeared. Bathsheba recovered and was taken in by her family. The cult of water's memory dissolved.

When someone asked me later if Johnnie had evolved beyond human to become an angel or a demon, I said I had no idea. What's beyond human? Nothing I've seen. I thought he went crazy a long time ago, and I should have told him so—not just to say I told him so, but to stop him. This is not a story about being right—I lost my friend. I don't know where or who he is anymore. Maybe after he was hurt, he was ready to move on, to a place where water did heal and remember everything it touched, where his parents danced on the air and woke him up each morning. I can understand the desire to see miracles. I just can't see what's not there.

Ben Bogart

Cormac McCarthy

I watched for you in Chicago,
grew anxious with the passing
of each white and balding head,
curled my toes in anticipation
at each flannel shirt,
counted the thin eyebrows, which
like yours,
frame the strained eyes of each writer
worth his weight in pretension,
turning silver,
documenting the unsaid, the unmentionable,
and what has come undone.
But you weren't there.

I stood patiently in Santa Fe supermarkets,
my eyes on the prunes,
waiting to shake you in your privacy,
to take back the twenty dollars you owe me,
and six hours of life,
to speak to you in quotation marks,
to trap you,
like a vegetable,
in the frozen foods.
No life or death,
just for personal observation.

I went out drinking with Stephen King,
and we played mini-golf,
talked about the Red Sox.
I almost hit him while driving home,
and he said that was alright,
that sometimes we imitate ourselves,
and love what we see in response.

Cormac,
Cormac whose name is really Charles,
but who felt more sinister than a Charles,
you I would truly love to see,
free from the keys of Hollywood,
typing into life cowboys,
who aren't so much cowboys
as businessmen. Or ransomed children,
or apocalyptic endings gone wrong.
If I found you, you wouldn't know me.
I'd become just another cowboy
in your books of cowboys.

Ben Bogart

Funeral Bells

Alone, I drop the needle on *Plastic Ono Band*
and with the whir of each revolution
I hear Lennon against the solemn,
grinding funeral bells
Mother, you had me, but I never had you
and I wonder what that day will be
like, knowing that some things
are always chosen for us.
Will it be a cloudy,
miserable bastard of a day? The kind
she hates, when the humidity reaches
into your shirt and sweats each drop
back out? Or will it be a grand,
gray irony of an affair, where the rain falls
upset, like a blues song, and washes
the feel of the day down spouts
and into empty roads.
That I could endure, for it's the heat
which really gets to her, a by-product
of the medication
and illness
and the stress of two young boys
and these aren't tragic,
they're just how things went.

Toni Mitchell

July Sparks

I feel ridiculous standing in Martha's festive kitchen in July, watching her fish out the powder blue scarf I know she's looking for. It was Jill's favorite; has become the one Martha always wears when we visit the memorial park. The bag on the floor next to her has a big stuffed animal lolling over its pinked edges—a white leopard with a plastic heart wedged between its paws. Leaning backward from the closet, Martha smiles with her delicately wrinkled mouth. She has large cheekbones and hazel eyes that glint like muddy water under the mesh of thick gray hair.

"Do you think she'll like it?"

"Martha, she'll love it."

A narrow crease surfaces in the center of Martha's forehead. She pauses, rummaging for something in my expression that I'm not ready to give up. "So serious today, Paul. What are you thinking?"

"Nothing I'm sharing," I say, hoping that a less direct, less painful tactic than telling her how I feel occurs to me.

She tips her head to the side and waves her polished fingernails. "Be that way."

She's light today, almost blithe, and that's encouraging. It should make this business easier. Sliding her feet into a pair of basil-brown loafers, she comes in a perfumed wave of vanilla and burnt cinnamon and weaves her plumpish arm through mine. "We should go. You know how she hates it when we're late."

I nod and stare at the blue mugs perched on the window-shelf above the sink. They're crammed with American flags that slump like orchids in a vase; sloppy and loose, nothing like the stiff bunch of roses I buy every time I'm here at what must be the smallest florist shop in Vermilion. It's the one about a block from Martha's house with the old man in green flannel jangling change behind the counter. He knew Jill before I did, which isn't saying much, but these people adopt you without questions, hold you close like you came with years of their friendship built in, and I don't mind that. He likes to tell me stories about Jill while he's emptying coin wrappers into the register, and I stare at his nametag and wonder why "Charlie" is so difficult to remember.

"She thought she was practical," he says, mining out the last obstinate quarter with his big-knuckled fingers. "Said it was stupid to buy flowers when you have to throw them out in two weeks."

Martha has hooked red chimes under a glittery banner outside her door, and they warble a few shrill notes as we pass them. The sky is metallic gray, like pewter, and there's a slow stream of blackbirds paddling through it. The broken dots of clouds are spread so that together they look like the cobblestone street over on Lorain Square, and a whitish sun stuck in the corner of the sky is all that's holding up the rain.

"You should come more often, you know? I could use the company." She's still smiling, and we walk to my Ford pickup where I open the passenger door for her. Down the street I can see a few star-spangled pinwheels turning in the wind, but none of the yards are quite as lit-up as Martha's. She has a wheelbarrow of red geraniums propped against her mailbox and American flag festoons draped around the porch.

On our first date, Jill told me she loved having her birthday right before the Fourth. She said when she was small she thought the fireworks were just for her and that, however odd it was, she found the idea appealing. There were certain parts of Jill that I did consider unusual, like the way she'd pay full price for a baseball ticket and then read through the whole game. Or this feline tendency she used to have where she'd fall asleep in the sunshine. But her affection for the Fourth of July has never been one of those parts. Somehow, it always fit her.

"Yeah, I should." I slide in next to Martha and pull the seatbelt over my chest. She knows I won't come any more than I already do, but it's a nice thing to say, so I say it and she folds her hand inside mine.

"You're getting to be like a son to me Paul, you know it?" I look at her and smile, but it feels awkward on my face. I stare ahead and anticipate the distance we'll have to go until Martha will start telling me the stories I've been hearing for a while now about Jill. They're always mixed up with new ones and in present tense, like Jill's listening, and like I've known her for years instead of the two and a half months she was my girlfriend.

They remind me of the first time I met Martha. Jill had slunk off to the kitchen, leaving me with this quietly officious woman I didn't know. She took me cover to cover through each of her scrapbooks. They were jacketed with yellow cloth, laid out tidily beneath the glass of her coffee table. To Martha, each picture was a bright, crackling moment in Jill's storyline. Nothing was insignificant. When she finished, she gave me a soft pat on the cheek and said, "Paul, you're a keeper."

Jill laughed at me later. I'd started the truck and honked goodbye to Martha, who waved from the porch. "I can't believe you sat through that," Jill said as she waved back.

I guess it's strange, but I prefer Martha's stories. Without them, there's just silence, she and I riding together like family, like two people someone might think love each other. There are times when I think we do love each other in an inexplicable way, but mostly all I can feel is this vague semblance of sadness, something ostensible, an emotion I want to have but can't.

On the corner of Niagara Road, there's a fireworks stand with a bright orange tarp sagging over it. A little girl in jelly shoes and pink shorts twirls a sparkler in the parking lot. Her silvery loops wilt into puffs of white smoke. As we drive past, Martha spreads her fingers against the window.

"Remember how much Jill spent on fireworks?"

I nod, trying to appear more congenial than I feel. "Yeah. She didn't know when to quit, did she?"

Martha laughs, giving my hand a squeeze. "No. I was always afraid she would blow herself up."

When I feel her head against my shoulder, I sigh and hope it sounds wistful. Martha has a stubbornness about her that makes you feel you ought to go her way and think things over later, that nothing could be worse than disappointing her. When she looks at me again, it's with an expression I don't deserve, like I'm a lighthouse that led her home once. I first saw it after Jill's funeral, and it has always made me feel like an imposter.

"How's Wanda?" She waits until we pull into the cemetery to ask this question. I think it's her way of telling me she just wants the short version. Instead of explaining that we're having problems, I tell her Wanda's fine, and that seems to be the answer she's looking for.

Martha moves quickly through the headstones, and I don't keep up. I wave at Sam, the groundskeeper, who's trimming the limbs of a purple thorn bush. Just across the highway from him, there's a tall gray house with a crooked fence sprawled around it. The fence is holding up a long piece of PVC pipe, and two small boys are lighting bottle rockets from the end of it. Sam doesn't seem to hear the drawn-out whistles and clattering pops. He and Martha have been friends longer than I've been alive. He shuffles over and cradles her elbow in his hands.

"Hey there, Martha." His blue eyes glisten like two pools of water in the middle of his sunburned face.

"Hi Sam. How are you?"

"Oh, the same. Not much changes here." Sam's shoes are glossy and black; they shift into a right angle when he stands still. "Good to see you, Paul." He pats me on the back and then the two amble ahead in a rhythm that's familiar to them, like how an old married couple might walk, and I'm more grateful than usual that he's here.

"Three years, Sam. Can you believe it?"

He wraps a bulky arm around Martha's shoulder. "Three Julys. It's not the same without her, is it?"

Martha rests her head in the space between Sam's shoulder and bristled jaw, which looks as though it was made for her. The red hedge trimmers dangling from his free hand remind me that Jill's flowers are still in my truck.

When I reach it, I can see my reflection frowning at me in the window, the overcast eyes and brown hair swept sideways, and I feel ridiculous again. I wonder how Jill would take this whole thing; how she would feel about some guy she dated for a couple months coming every year with her mom to stare at her stone. Not that we weren't friends. With more time, we could've been good friends. I liked the way she always giggled at everything, as if she had one up on the world. When I met her, she was sitting in the row in front of me at Jacob's Field reading a book of Ginsberg's poetry. She had dark brown eyes and waist-length hair. She said the print was right side up, the cover upside down, and she liked the fluke. I didn't notice. The book didn't interest me. It was the top of the ninth and the Indians were down by five, so I was ready for a distraction, particularly an attractive one.

"I think they still have a chance," I'd said facetiously.

"Me too. This next guy's going to hit a grand slam." She chuckled and offered me the empty seat next to her, and at the time that was all I wanted. I wasn't sure what I wanted with her the night Martha called me about the wreck, Jill and a few of her friends driving a little too fast. I guess we were in that place of inertia where you think you could be more, but you have to wait on time, so you practice the physical works while the mental ones catch up.

My keys manage a subdued clink on their way out of my pocket, and as I climb into the truck I set the flowers on the passenger seat. Sam could take Martha home. She'd be okay eventually. It won't exactly be subtle, but it might be better than indulging this clumsy half-pretense. I expect her to come hurrying over when I start the engine, but when I do there's only me, and I think back to Wanda standing in our bathroom in a short white T-shirt while I grappled with my tie.

"What'll this make it now, Paul? Three years?" Wanda's arms were folded over her small breasts. She never wore a bra.

"Well, do you see an alternative?" I turned from the water-splattered mirror to face her. "Would you like me to tell her to get over it?"

A strand of Wanda's bright blond hair fell across her face as she waved an arm in exasperation. Her eyes, green and almost square-shaped, perceptibly darkened when she grabbed a comb from the sink and worked it with quick, angry thrusts. "Don't make me out to be the heavy, here. If this is going to work, if *we* are going to work, *you* have to end this. And you know it. You're with me now. Not Jill. And not Martha."

"Martha expects something from me."

"It's different for her. Jill was her daughter. You knew her for what, a month? She can't expect you to feel the same thing."

146

"I know that. I'm just trying to work this out."

"Paul, there's nothing left to work out."

I gripped Wanda's waist and tried to push past her, catching the sweet smell of clean linen and coconut. "Just forget it, okay? I'll be back in a few hours."

She clutched my shirtsleeve and pulled me to her, scowling at my tie. The soft tap of her comb against the sink and the gentle tug of her fingers at my collar were somehow grounding. "Paul, please try to talk to her. You can't do this forever."

"I know."

The words were more of a peace offering than a promise, but Wanda is right about this. It isn't something built to last. I stare at the red bouquet pouting on the seat next to me and realize I'm only kidding myself. I'm not going anywhere until I talk to Martha. I turn off the truck.

She's putting up the stuffed leopard for Jill when I get back. Her smile is a little muddled, and she's still leaning heavily on Sam's arm. I place the roses next to the leopard and feel the sudden tightening of her fingers around my wrist.

"The flowers really are beautiful, Paul. Jill loves them, always, I know." I nod, watching our three shadows converge over Jill's headstone.

"You going to stay awhile?" Sam's booming voice seems to dissipate in the calm graveyard, giving way to the erratic shrieks of the boys behind their pipe. The loudest of them is on his back, holding his stomach and laughing wildly into the air. The other is blowing fiercely on his hand and wagging it back and forth. "Paul?"

"I don't think so." I turn to see that Sam's whiskered face has gathered itself into one immense grin. "I promised Wanda I wouldn't be late."

Martha's hand slips downward into mine. "Next year, then?"

When she looks at me, I turn to Jill's blue-specked stone with its closely cropped beard of ivy. I like to think I loved Jill, at least in some capacity, to think that love is a bit like a rental, a place you let people come and live, that ultimately belongs to you. But maybe whether or not those people stay is more than just a decision you make for yourself. Maybe love is a little less deliberate.

"Martha, I don't think I can make it next year."

She frowns at me for a few seconds, and her full lower lip puckers when she tries to smile. "I didn't know you planned that far ahead."

"That's not what I mean."

She nods. "I know what you mean."

"I'm sorry, Martha."

"Is it Wanda?"

I shove a hand into my dress pant pocket and finger one of my keys. "No, it's not Wanda. It's me."

"What about Jill?"

Sam braces Martha's shoulders in his great mitt-like hands. His eyes are passive when they meet mine, unlike Martha's, which flicker up at me in confusion. "You loved her, didn't you Paul?"

"I'm grateful for the time I had with her," I say, but it sounds awful, like something I once said to a dealer when I returned the '64 Corvette Stingray I test-drove. "There just wasn't enough of it, Martha."

"I know," she says softly, but for a different reason, I think. A small smile turns up the corners of her mouth, and I see it again, that quick flame of trust in her eyes that has no right to be there, that I haven't earned, like I'm someone she knows she can always depend on. She holds out her hand, and when I take it I wonder if it wouldn't be so bad to become that person. "Will you still come and see *me*?"

I imagine Martha sitting across from me at the Lakeside Café, her smooth hands folded on the table as we attempt a conversation. Somehow, I can't make her lips move without putting Jill's name in them. "I don't know."

She nods once, keeping her eyes downward. There's a translucent string of dampness under each one. Sam gives me a benign glance and pulls a checkered handkerchief from his pocket. His quick familiarity with the gesture is vindicating. I want to believe this is something he's seen before, that he's just been waiting for his moment.

When they continue their slow step, I watch the space spread out between us, feeling colder and heavier inside than I did this morning in Martha's kitchen. I stare at the garish red heart fixed between the paws of Jill's leopard and wonder what Wanda's doing now. I wonder if she's still annoyed with me or if she's waiting on the veranda in her gray plaid robe and T-shirt, the ends of her damp hair leaving water trails along the pages of those math puzzles she likes so much. It's only a forty-five minute drive back to Cleveland, but this place always feels farther out than it really is, like a giant disconnection that makes you believe nothing came before or after. And for some reason, I'm glad I have the thought of Wanda to remind me that there's more than this indistinct sadness and the sputtering of a few bottle rockets being fired off before the Fourth.

D. GILSON

Holding My Breath

For Esther Gilson

Grandma and I walk through the woods near her house
and I realize I don't really know this woman. Her name is
Esther which is epic but she's just a girl from Iowa who
married Lyman, moved to southern Arkansas, opened up a
flea market, and hated every female member of her family. We walk these woods because I have upset Lyman, who
doesn't appreciate his grandson putting on a one-man version of *South Pacific* on his low brick hearth. We walk these
woods and I don't know who she is, which is fine because
she doesn't know who I am either. She is dying here, a slow
death of the brain she tells me—me being eight—that
makes her forget some things from time to time and will
eventually make her forget how to breathe. This is funny,
forgetting how to breathe, and I hold my breathe as she re-
lates the story of the first time she made love—it was in her
father's cornfield, not with Lyman, which she recommends
is the way to go because we ain't meant to be with only one
person in our lives and I don't know about all that yet but
realize this is something I should remember. She turns to
me, asks who I am again—just a kid, Esther, just a kid—the
world spins faster and faster beneath our feet.

D. GILSON

Hearth, Hearth

No one told me the place had been demolished.
Once here a house stood, a farmhouse on this
country road and no one knew what it meant

to me. I sure as hell didn't. I pulled over and got out
of the car, ran my hands along a stone foundation
that had bore four small bedrooms, children, an evolving

kitchen, cupboard and stoneware, cornmeal, flour, barley,
great room, cellar, stove, hearth, hearth, stairs.
The farmer and his wife laid these floorboards,

now in a pile at my feet, nails haphazardly bent here
and there. I thumb the grain of one, pray it to rot
into that new life, to become that bit of earth.

MARIE SCHURK

Ice Rain

Like more cautious raindrops
single notes hit white concrete,

a rooftop, or a slight tree branch
lingering in an icy state, but it is water

a part of ourselves: sealed together,
yet vulnerable. Specks innocently mimic

our timid personalities, and the gradual
learners at a classroom. Melting shells

seep in airy surroundings, contribute
with an unrecognized significance.

Scattered entities feed a new spring
mocking our own emergent families

but each drop of a seemingly similar task
reaches a different pore in the earth.

KINSLEY STOCUM

A Long Walk with My Mother

There's one in every generation,
she panted out
and unintentionally sealed my fate.

We took a broad, sloping curve
with practiced strides,
our legs swinging on well-oiled hips,

our thigh muscles bunching to bring
knees and calves and soft leather shoes
up and down again on the unlined pavement,

the shock from the road filtered out
through a long chain of connecting bones—
we glided, rather than bounced.

My uncle had a questionable war wound,
she continued, *you know, in* that *area*
that kept him from getting married.

Our breath poured out in billowing
white puffs as the cold
air went burning through our lungs

in and out, and our arms swung
and swung and propelled us forward
as we flew alone in the dusk,

the creeping dark filled with the voices
of crickets and peep frogs and mothers
and a daughter gathering the truths of her life.

And my cousin Liz, who lived
and worked and traveled
and died alone with her family, she added.

We flicked on our flashlights
as the headlights of a Ford flooded
our vision and forced us off the road,

our breasts heaving on top
of expanding lungs
and our stomachs sucking in.

III. From Points Beyond

NIKKI SETTELMEYER, TRANSLATOR

"El Fantasma" ("The Vision")
by Hernán Migoya

He would find rats the size of horses and
maybe he'd even come across a human skeleton.
It was a long shot but if he found that
if he found that, he would be rich,
incredibly rich with mysteries
—*Chico de Madrid*, Ignacio Aldecoa

"The night said you were mine."
—*El gato que está triste y azul*, Toto Savio

"The eye always wins."
—Walerian Borowczyk

This is important, so listen:

On planet Earth, there lives a boy named Asdrúbal who cannot close both eyes at once. He can only blink one eye at a time.

Bizarre, right? But how lucky for me.

In 1956, a dimwitted redhead named Sue Landford had the same idea, to put this story into writing in a tidy essay for her English professor at Hoboken Institute in New Jersey. But lucky for me, the lively Lolita was paying more attention to the risqué faces and lip gestures of the naughty new boy in class. In the end, with her head in the clouds—or something like that—the idea went out the window, whisked away by the new boy's sighs which were totally unconscious and really had nothing at all to do with her. When it came time to put pen to paper, Sue opted, instead, to write a glorified autobiography, a work that hasn't yet made its way into the annals of literature.

Consequently, I sincerely believe that this story of Asdrúbal is one hundred percent original. Now, I know a person can never really be one hundred percent sure of anything, but, everything has already been written . . . .

I'm getting off track. As I was saying, Asdrúbal has to blink with one eye at a time: first one, then the other. Try to do it yourself: first the other, then the one. Feels awkward, right? As a result, Asdrúbal found himself, one way or another, always having one eye open. He was always seeing something, at all times. Constantly.

Now, I know that blinking really doesn't cause a major loss of vision, if any at all. Our eyelid falls so fast, the eye barely registers a thing; a flicker, a single frame in a film reel, a blink (in the end, it is what it is) in the electric current, practically undetected. We don't usually notice such involuntary phenomena, but unfortunately, other people notice. Imagine a well-meaning classmate trying to maintain eye contact with Asdrúbal: one eye coming, the other going. The eyes of this individual unconsciously following the alternating movement—now one, now the other—of Asdrúbal's eyes, unable to settle on only one.[1] He or she will surely be ashamed and pity the poor defective boy. Imagine poor Asdrúbal in the school yard, trying to hold an age-appropriate conversation, insecure and visually stuttering in front of his classmates, those elegant synchronized dual blinkers.

When the left falls, the right rises, and when the left rises, the right falls.

---

[1] Because—and I feel shameful even bringing it up—while we don't always notice it, or it seems completely contrary, when we look into a someone's eyes, face to face, it's impossible to focus on each eye at the same time and we can't look at both of them at once, no matter how hard we concentrate! In reality, we NEVER look at both eyes! Because of a mere biological factor; how unromantic, right?: "I looked into her eye and then I looked into the other one, and I said, I love you." Ugh!

How much more he will suffer if, on top of all this, the boys in his class are inclined to teasing and ridicule, and the girls snub any supposed physical defect, and surely this is how it is at his school. That's the way it has been and the way it always will be in our schools, where "normal" is a most admirable trait during those insecure childhood years and any exception to the norm—to normality—is punished with the most cruel jeering and humiliation.

Asdrúbal's nickname is Clock, a gift from his class. When he passes a fellow student, he invariably hears "tick-tock, tick-tock," followed by unmistakable muffled laughter.

It won't be difficult to understand the loneliness Asdrúbal sees himself doomed to, if at some time you've felt alone—and who's never felt alone, no matter what sex, species or planet you belong to? The loneliness surrounds him every day of his life, and never changes or varies, no matter how much he tick-tocks.

Trapped by his crystal balls, his meaty marbles, Asdrúbal keeps a distance from his cruel classmates. And as if reclaiming the organic being of his eyes, delighting in his misfortune, he marks the rhythm of his steps with the imaginary tick-tock that regulates the rise and fall of his eyelids. Tick, one step, tock, another. Tick . . .

Now, this is not a case of a boy not getting enough love at home. His mother loves him with vehement resolve. True, he can't count on a father's love, because, due to circumstances that, at his age, are inconceivable, he's never known his father. What he does know is that it could have been worse: he could have been born the child of an abusive father—there are certainly many of them around—like some of the notorious battered children in his own class who are, in turn, merciless to their classmates. They are especially mean to Asdrúbal, and still he only blames their cruelty on the malicious father. Asdrúbal's mother works in the post office, weighing packages and sticking stamps, and she devotes the few remaining hours of the day to caring for her son and to lying on the couch, sighing, exhausted.

His mother, of course, noticed the abnormal blinking immediately, as soon as it began several years ago. Several years for Asdrúbal, that is, not for us. As a panic-stricken mother who lives only for her child, whose existence depends entirely on the child's existence, she rushed him to the doctor, afraid that her son was suffering a grave problem and the strange blinking was merely a symptom of some greater incurable illness announcing its presence—a strange way of making itself known—in Asdrúbal's organism. So when the doctor, after months of tests and examinations, diagnosed her son's supposed mystery illness as no more than a pure and innocuous muscular inability to synchronize the closing of the eyelids, the woman was wholeheartedly relieved. A little too relieved, if I'm completely honest, because over time, for Asdrúbal, not being able to close his eyes in tandem, has become a severe affliction. But for his mother, it's NOTHING: because he's her son and because she loves him exactly as he is, the whole world should love him too, just as he is. Oh, these mothers who love their children so much they don't even recognize an actual affliction.

Once in a while, let it be known, Asdrúbal has walked in to find his mother crying. She'll hide her face and pretend to be dusting a shelf, but he knows. Asdrúbal has only cried once that he remembers. Not at birth; that doesn't count. He can't remember the reason, but because he couldn't close his eyes to shed a decent tear, the experience was deprived of any comforting effect and instead turned into a hideous and terrifying experience as his eyes seemed to be drowning in a flood. He decided he would never cry again. And he has kept this promise.

At that age when the only thing that matters is what other people think—and no one can escape it—Asdrúbal tried a thousand ways to conceal his defect—let's call it that just for once, so not to swell the ranks of the intolerant torturers. With patience and skill, he practiced quickly closing his eyelids, one right after the other, one right on the heels of the other, two planes called to action and willing to perform a stealthy drop, matched in time with only a microsecond's difference. But as soon as the second eyelid lowered, the first had risen. The effect was even more bizarre than the usual bizarreness, because to anyone else's eyes, his appeared to be executing syncopated winking, which caused even more hysterical outbursts all around him. As soon as the other children noticed, they didn't hold back a thing—including angry wads of spit from the girls.

Though minute, visual interruption happens to be necessary for the moisturization and preservation of the eye and relief of ocular irritation. The rest of us disengage from reality for a number of hours each day during a restful dream—but not Asdrúbal. Unable to administer a synchronized descent of the eyelids, Asdrúbal is forced to shut down one eye, only to liberate the other, incapable of simultaneously lowering both sets of blinds that cut the rest of us off from the exhausting outside world. The rest of us surrender to the affections of an obscure universe that loves us or frightens us, but either way, always silently promises to return us unharmed to the place of departure. For Asdrúbal, even sleep is punishment.

One afternoon, Asdrúbal discovered that his mother was a regular consumer of sleeping pills. He discovered this when he asked her why she took so many red pills. (The color red bothers him; he doesn't know why, it's just part of his make-up. Just like some people don't like the looks of white mulberry leaves, the feel of peach skin, or a stranger's sweat.) His mother gave a reasonable answer. Asdrúbal asked if he too could take them. His mother said no, "They aren't for children," she said. "If you take too many you could go to sleep forever and never wake up."

160

"Like papa?"

This time his mother didn't answer.

Let's take a look at how Asdrúbal sleeps. It takes over an hour to accomplish, and it's only after he has forgotten about the unrelenting tick-tock and surrenders to it, the way a guinea pig surrenders itself to the hypnotic tick-tocking of a watch, even if it's the only sound disturbing the silence of the cage. It is only then that he manages to fall asleep and calm his spirit. And thus the moment arrives when Asdrúbal, commanded by his exhausted body, lets himself go and releases his eyelids to their proper spheres, leaving them to their own will—of which they have none—to rise and fall tiredly, directed only by each eye's fundamental instinct for survival.

The neglected and aimless eyelids, by free will of the organism, reluctantly slow down, and move with exasperating lethargy, like tired wings beating, or heavy paddles maneuvered by a dying oarsman, and sluggish progression, like the crawl of a slug or the soft throbbing of a mollusk, to the point that the only inherent request of the open eye, managed by the body's own biological mechanism, like a cerebral response to a progressive burning sensation, is to pull the selfish curtain and secure it, ipso facto, while the neighboring curtain rises again to re-admit the world's stage without disturbing the child's rest in any way.

And what does Asdrúbal see through the open eye appointed to said world's stage?

I belong to a certain stock of human beings who, for all that has been said about the benefits of practicing good posture for the vertebral column and for the rest of the organism, have never been able to sleep lying on their backs, in other words, horizontally, face-up, upon the neck, back, buttocks and legs, supported on top of the mattress and forming a straight line parallel to the bedroom walls. Therefore, it is impossible for me to imagine Asdrúbal sleeping in such a position and involuntarily visualizing the ceiling, now with one eye, now with the other.

For this reason, after minor speculation, I have decided to put him in the easiest position, the most common for humanity. Asdrúbal winds down and sleeps with simultaneous comfort and apprehension, lying on his side, facing one of the concrete walls of his bedroom and the window that looks across the courtyard to the apartments of his noisy neighbors, who don't intrude—thank God—in this story.

And so, Asdrúbal's eyes are confronted with alternating views: a segment of wall—but not the ceiling—and an aluminum framed window, and the empty other half of the bed.

Do these images interfere with Asdrúbal's rest or disturb perhaps the sweet affair of his mind, spellbound in the fumes of comforting lethargy? No, not even close. Not without effort anyway.

Yes, it's true that, thanks to the inescapable, unending vision of Asdrúbal's eyes, the unremitting images always accompany his nocturnal journey. But they do so on another level. Sometimes Asdrúbal even forgets about them, and that barren scenery transforms into a curtain and backdrop. And on some of these occasions, the bleak scenery even turns into a one-dimensional screen where the other scenery, the fantastic, exotic, dream scenery, is projected. There, he is admired and fearless. On rare occasion, the screen interferes and prevails in his head, waking him and forcing him to abandon his amazing kingdom, forcing him to see, to see another damn time, a segment of the wall—but not the ceiling—and the aluminum framed window, and the empty other half of the bed. A segment of bare white wall, the aluminum framed window, always cold and un-inspirational, and the other half of the bed, always empty, no one at his side: no one to love him.

Oh, don't give me that a-mother's-love-is-all-you-need story. Were you never a child, you crusty old goat?

Loneliness surrounds the child who can't close both eyes at the same time. He is relentlessly surrounded, but most of all, during the night. And there's nothing he can do to shut his eyes to this loneliness. *Tick-tock, tick-tock.* Sometimes it's *tock-tock.* The loneliness knocking over and over on the door, demanding his partial notice.

But things have changed. Because for two or three months now, Asdrúbal has been having the same dream.

Well, it isn't *exactly* the same dream. It would be more accurate to say that he dreams about the same person.

He doesn't know who she is. He's never met her. He's never seen her (I mean, in real life). Yes, you've guessed it: He's got a dreamgirl. An adorable blonde girl. Maybe an angel. Angelic she is, without a doubt.

The fascinating thing about all of this is that he doesn't even know if he's really dreaming.

Why do I say that? Well, hang onto your chair because what I'm about to tell you is tricky and it may take a while to explain: in Asdrúbal's dream, when the girl appears, there is no IMAGINARY SCENERY. (Suck on that, Sue Landford!)

Understand? Wait, I'll try to explain a little better (ugh, this is hard, so pay attention): what I mean to say is that there is no scenery in Asdrúbal's head interfering with what his eyes capture each night as they alternately open and close. That is, if we're talking about a distinct scenery. But it could be that the scenery where the little girl appears is the same, detail for detail, as what Asdrúbal sees with his eyes!

So, both are superimposed, but they're identical. Probability full of improbability, obviously; unconsciously, his imaginary scenery would have to replace, with a slight change in perception, the actual scene that tortures each eye.

But let's not spoil the party before it begins and let's not sabotage our own attempts at creating splendor.

Asdrúbal is utterly beside himself in love.

It couldn't be any other way: he doesn't know where she's from, her place of origin, but she is adorable, as I've already mentioned. Adorable. Of course, the poor child can't possibly know, and if he does know, he can't accept that she is only a creation of his own mind, of his imagination run rampant, runaway in the witching hour; freed are the reigns of his most basic being, and why not, of his soul. He couldn't accept, if it were explained to him, that the object of his adoration only signifies a typical diversion, a distraction on behalf of a sensible mind, his sensible mind, desperate for the love and affection of a divine being: for the love of someone superior to his mother and greater than himself, someone who can convince him that his misfortune has some purpose, that his life is worth the suffering. Someone who controls his destiny. Asdrúbal couldn't accept that his beloved is a mute projection of his subconscious because when he dreams, she, the girl, is lying right there at his side, breathing, not going anywhere. And she has come to him precisely because he is the way he is.

It isn't difficult to understand why Asdrúbal believes in her existence. When he sleeps, the little nymph appears vibrant at his side, at his very side, materialized on top of the covers, the white sheet, that portion of the mattress that had been cold and empty until now. The girl doesn't say anything: he looks at her and smiles, his pupils dilated in the gentle light, but sufficient to make her out, lying on his bed, carelessly reclining on his poly-blend bedspread, which has to cause discomfort and maybe even itchiness after a while. In a white dress stamped with roses of every color except pink, there she is, eye candy, just within reach. His arms long to embrace her, to hold her. They could, but they don't. He suspects deep down that he's afraid to reach out his hands and try to touch her, for fear the fantasy will be exposed. Whatever the reason, the fact remains: he never hugs her. He only looks at her, with one eye, now the other, one lid

164

ascending, the ascending lid and the descending lid, now one, now the other, and she is always there, virtually motionless, barely swayed by his altering point of view, that sweet eternal undulation that puts order and happiness in his restlessness.

But obviously, her presence is not eternal after all. When Asdrúbal least expects it, when he is admiring her, engrossed with both eyes to admire her all the more, the girl suddenly vanishes into the air, fades to translucence: the bedroom scenery takes over from there. Terrified, the sleeping Asdrúbal thinks the girl has only disappeared from his sight and closes the eye he thinks she's disappeared from. Sometimes he's right, sometimes he's wrong. Even if he's right, the happiness still doesn't last. Because when the open eye, seeking respite, abruptly demands to close, the relieving eye still can't locate the darling, and neither can the other when it immediately reopens: she has been vaporized and only the pitiful bed remains, an image superimposed or real.

A minute passes and Asdrúbal realizes he's awake. His proof is in the irritation of his eyes, reddened by exertion.

Like clockwork, the girl reappears the following night. On certain occasions, when the previous night was frustrating, beyond frustrating, Asdrúbal tries to speak to his phantom girlfriend. He tries to peel his lips apart and whisper some charming expression, something he's never before had the opportunity to say. But in those moments his mouth doesn't respond, as if it had become infected with the same sort of self-government as his eyelids, deciding to immobilize and fall perpetually silent.

Having said this, I should also make it clear that the girl doesn't seem bothered in the least.

So what's she like? Imagine total relaxation. Absolute happiness. She's reminiscent of something you sense you might've intuitively felt, but you're not sure if you *really* felt it. If you saw her (and in your case she could take any form or incarnation), you'd immediately say: "Oh, now I remember! Now I know why I'm always caught up feeling unhappy and irritable, longing for who-knows-what. How unlucky for me! Somehow, my primal being remembers what I lost at the starting line: it was this. . .''

And so Asdrúbal's nights pass, marked by two eyelids on uncoordinated rotating shifts, in the company of a girl who fills his empty hours with affection and importance.

Asdrúbal hasn't cried other than the one time, as I've already mentioned, but recently something has begun to change in him. The first days, following the first nights sleeping in the company of the girl, he was surprisingly vivacious and cheerful, setting aside his usual passive and apathetic self. Even his mother noticed the change, mistakenly attributing it to her son's growing up; breaking out of his shell, if you will.

But in more recent days, Asdrúbal has come to replace that carefree enthusiasm with an increasing irritability. Any little thing can set him off—ask his mother. It's not just that he's aloof and anti-social. He is beginning to snap back with spiteful remarks. And he throws outrageous tantrums when Mamá serves spinach omelets yet again, even though he has told her a thousand times that he doesn't like them, and for the thousandth time she is surprised.

Yesterday, for example, he threw his plate on the floor.

Asdrúbal feels he's been cheated. Yes, he's always felt this way, so he should be used to it. I know, but try telling him that. If you'll allow me to speak on his behalf for just a moment, I will argue in his defense that this feeling, frankly, is of a different caliber, and the boy has certain justification for his cynical attitude: before, Asdrúbal only wanted to assimilate into the world and resign himself to a relatively tolerable life where the other mortals accept him just the way he is. Now Asdrúbal knows what happiness is, he has experienced it, even if only a little, and he can't imagine giving it up or accepting that the source of his happiness doesn't belong to the real world.

We all give in or give up sooner or later, this is true. We bury the memory of something, some thing, of what or if it ever really *was*, we are not sure, but we bury the memory until there is only a trace of a glorious past that couldn't possibly have ever existed. But it existed. And Asdrúbal can't bear waking up each morning and watching as his darling disappears from his eyes and from his bed.

Each morning he spends more time lying there. But it hasn't done any good since she only appears in the deepest phase of sleep, when Asdrúbal has already given up waiting and someone else decides that it's time for her to appear to him.

So this week he has employed a new approach. Instead of investing more fruitless time in bed, he has asked his mother to enroll him in soccer, even though he knows his companions don't want him there. But he isn't doing it to win the favor and esteem of the other boys who have rejected him until now. How surprised they are to see Clock running and jumping and skipping around the ball like a titan.

And why is he making such an effort if his intention isn't to be accepted by his classmates? They don't even matter anymore. He couldn't care less about them.

He wants to come home, worn out and exhausted, take a relaxing shower and go to bed, completely drained, to dream, dream, dream.

And his eyes can rise and fall, rise and fall, rise and fall.

Whatever.

I suppose you've already predicted the outcome of this story.

As have I. And I only realized recently, so don't be so sure of yourself. It came to me when I decided that the girl would appear in the same background that Asdrúbal's eyes mull over each night.

It's a beautiful ending, but sad. I like sad endings.

Sad but true.

Asdrúbal has already given up trying to bring his darling to reality. He's not completely conscious of it either, since it has been he who has been moving further away, little by little, from reality, and now he wants nothing to do with it at all.

Asdrúbal remembers what his mother told him about the pills she takes to fall asleep. He recalls perfectly which ones they were: the ones that boast that abhorrent color.

Asdrúbal pilfers the bottle of pills, and ten minutes after saying goodnight to Mamá, takes advantage of an unexpected trip to the bathroom. Instead of peeing, he takes out the pills and looks at them one by one, to see them from the individual perspective of his two eyes, first with one side, then with the other: through the first eye they're shiny; through the second they have a dull and rough finish. He takes the pills, two at a time until he has taken twenty. Seriously, ceremoniously, he wolfs them down and swallows water from the faucet.

Stuffed full of narcotics, Asdrúbal returns to his bedroom and lies down on his side to wait for the pills to take effect.

Asdrúbal smiles with anticipation, waiting to fall asleep.

Asdrúbal falls asleep without knowing he's sleeping. He sees her there, in front of him, and she returns his gaze. She is so pretty, so beautiful and precious and adorable and kissable and so completely his that Asdrúbal wants to cry for the first time out of sheer joy. Because when he made the decision to never again shed a tear, he didn't consider that sometimes we also cry for joy. Or maybe he didn't even know. What a wonderful discovery!

So he cries, he weeps in his sleep, fearing the tears will forever obscure his object of affection. But she isn't obscured. Only blurred.

When the crying is over, she clears. Still there. She never left and she's never going to leave. She'll never allow Asdrúbal to be alone again.

Asdrúbal smiles, because he knows that now, nothing can spoil his happiness.

Asdrúbal only has eyes for her. One and the other. Right?

Asdrúbal doesn't even notice that he's already been looking at her for over an hour with the same, single eye.

The other has closed and hasn't opened again.

WAWAN EKO YULIANTO, TRANSLATOR

"The Mandarin Fireflies"
by Seno Gumira Ajidarma

There, in the town where the rainbow never fades, nobody thinks the way Sukab does. He runs a firefly farm. From the top of the hill, his farm, near the sea, gives off light, like a spotlight. It's a yellowish green, or greenish yellow, phosphorescent beam. Tourists strolling by the sea at night are amazed to see such a brilliant light.

"What light is that?"

"Oh, that's the light from Sukab's firefly farm."

"Firefly farm?"

"That's right, firefly farm. Nobody in this town thinks the way he does."

The species of fireflies that Sukab raises is not an ordinary one, but grown from the nail clippings of Chinese Mandarins. It is believed that the Mandarins always keep their nail clippings. When they die, their nail clippings are buried with them. The night after they are buried, those small nail fragments turn into fireflies, and they fly out, making the deep dark night in the graveyard bright. Fireflies around the graveyard look as beautiful and sweet as the heart of a good man that shines through the dark.

"Fireflies, venturing the woods of pain . . ."

People usually hear Sukab singing this lightly to his guitar in front of his farm. Tourists who are passing his place always stop because they are charmed by the yellowish green or greenish yellow light beaming to the sky, like a column of light thrown up by archangels. Ships that pass far away on the sea use it to steer by, as some kind of special lighthouse.

"Ladies and Gentlemen, to the north is a column of light, which means we're passing the town where the rainbow never fades. That yellowish green or greenish yellow light beaming to the sky comes from a firefly farm. For your information, if you want to set up a firefly farm in your country, you should know that only fireflies from the nail clippings of the Mandarins can be that bright. The night after their burial, fireflies that come from the nail clippings preserved throughout life, from infancy to death, will fly out from the underground. Ladies and Gentlemen . . ."

It began during a crisis, when life was hard and happiness became rare. People suffered, and hard work did not earn them anything. Sukab was thinking about all these when a firefly passed before his face, blinking, as if surrendering. Sukab snatched it, kept it in a small pill bottle, covered it with a patch of netting, and tied a rubber band around to secure it. All alone, deep in thought, he meditated on the firefly, and realized how the insect gave a light in the dark. Suddenly, he forgot about his useless life.

That night he went to the graveyard of the Mandarins on the hillside. It was an old graveyard, underneath which were buried the Mandarins from the distant past. Years and years back, in the town where the rainbow never fades, the Mandarins were hunted as if they were creatures that should be exterminated and were not supposed to live on Earth. They were slaughtered like animals, none were left, despite the fact that they were the ones who had furthered trade in that town. People said that when the massacre took place, the rainbow, which had never faded, for the first time in history did fade and even disappeared. Only after people realized that they were wrong, and regretted what they had done, and performed a mass repentance ceremony, the rainbow reappeared. The rainbow that never fades is another major town attraction. Tourists come to touch the rainbow, but of course they can't touch anything because the rainbow is not a wall, but light.

It was the story about those massacred Mandarins that made Sukab decide to move and live in that coastal town. He likes climbing up the hill where the massacre victims are buried. There he sees a thousand fireflies blinking in the dark, flying around like some dance from the dreamland.

"Perhaps these are the fireflies that come from the nail clippings of the dead Mandarins," he thought, "their brightness is not an ordinary light of fireflies, it's an enlightening brightness."

At first, Sukab only set a small table outside of his hut, and put five pill bottles on it, each containing a firefly that gave off a brightness in the dark.

One of the passing tourists became interested.

"What's this?"

"Fireflies."

"What's a firefly?"

"A kind of small insect that flies around in the fields."

"Aha! The one with a phosphorescent glow?"

"That's it! Here they are."

"Why sell them?"

"Who knows? You want to buy one? You don't have fireflies in Scandinavia, right? Besides, these are not ordinary fireflies."

Then Sukab told the story about the Mandarin people's nail clippings. It turned out that the story made people buy his fireflies, and Sukab could establish a firefly farm whose beam became a sky-supporting column. The arrival of foreigners who were enchanted by that story saved the town from a long economic downturn. Any souvenir related to the story quickly sells. True enough, in the town where the rainbow never fades there are various attractions that bring in tourists who come for anything from surfing to visiting sacred caves. However, since the economic downturn, political riots sprang up, there was bloodshed everywhere, and the number of tourists decreased. It was Sukab's firefly farm that emerged as the major industry to compete with those from other tourist towns, and in fact the seaside town where the rainbow never fades regained its prosperity.

One unexpected day, a Chinese Mandarin came to the town alone. He was a scholar who was always very curious about the history of his race, and therefore interested in the story about the Mandarin fireflies, which come from nail clippings. Sukab served him *arak* wine, but this man did not get drunk easily.

"So, Mr. Sukab, you catch fireflies that fly around the graveyard?"

"Yes, then I farm them."

"But your fireflies are so much different from the ordinary ones found in the fields. Your fireflies are not the kind described in encyclopedias. We can't find their scientific name. A billion ordinary fireflies wouldn't be strong enough to create a sky-supporting column of light, and ordinary fireflies flicker about at night only to be found dead in the morning, while your fireflies can enlighten hearts lost in the darkness."

"Come on, Mr. Udin Mandarin, don't exaggerate."

"I think you understand, Mr. Sukab, that I'm not exaggerating. Is it really possible to breed mystical fireflies from the Mandarins' nail clippings? Your fireflies are not biological insects, they're mystical. My question is, what kind of treatment do you give them as farm animals? They aren't the kind of fireflies that can be bred. Those fireflies are from nail clippings. They come out of the grave at night digging up through the ground. Are they breedable?"

"Mr. Udin Mandarin, I'm just a simple man, I don't think with my head. I only follow what my heart says. I never ask myself those questions. I don't even know what you mean."

"My question is, if you run out of those nail-clipping fireflies, which in fact cannot be bred, what will you do?"

Sukab studied his guest. He was an educated Mandarin, and it was very clear that he never did manual labor. His fingers were well-groomed and looked soft, like a lady's. His nails were rather long, but very clean, almost as clear as calm water in the pond.

"Mr. Udin Mandarin, Sir, how do you expect me to answer such a question about something I never do?"

One night, after interviewing a lot of people about the fireflies with the same questions he had asked Sukab, the Mandarin scholar went to the hill where the Mandarins were buried. He could see the Mandarins' graves on the hillside, facing the sea. The rustling of the wind was very distinct, and he could hear the roaring waves that sounded as if they were chasing one another before crashing on the beach. As if they were telling a story. He imagined how, in the grave, the Mandarins were sitting around staring at the sea, chatting with the wind that brought them news from around the world.

He had heard how the Mandarins had been killed, raped, and slaughtered. He imagined how the nail clippings buried along with them turned into fireflies, pushed up through the ground, and flew around flickering as lights in the dark.

But there were not any fireflies that night. The world was dark, and he could not even see the moon and stars in the sky.

"What a dark world," the Mandarin scholar thought. The sky supporting beam was the only light seen from where he was sitting. It was a yellowish green, greenish yellow phosphorescent beam. He could barely understand how the Mandarins' nail clippings could turn into fireflies that created such a world-wonder light.

"Why can't this world be ordinary, without incredible stories?" he thought again. "Even if the story is *not* incred-

174

ible, who would have had the chance to put the nail clippings into the grave? Weren't *all* the Mandarins in town slaughtered? Who took care of their dead bodies? Did they always carry the nail clippings everywhere they went?"

As a Mandarin who was used to traveling around the world, he never kept his nail clippings.

The rustling of the wind from the sea sounded like Requiem.

"Mr. Udin Mandarin," someone called.

Behind a patch of tall grasses, he saw black figures around the hill, circling him.

Each was holding a saber in his hand.

In his hut, Sukab was singing lightly.

Fireflies, venturing through the woods of pain . . .

THOM SATTERLEE, TRANSLATOR

Poetry
by Per Aage Brandt

i sneen efterlader man spor, indtil den store sorte
sneskraber kommer buldrende og gør vejen bred,
så kan man altid prøve igen, indtil osv., indtil det
bliver forår, og man i øvrigt snarere svæver over
det nyrejste græs som en guldsmed og en kolibri,
de har aldrig sat deres støvler i den substans, der
her er tale om; for nu er man kun en slags grafik
på nethinden, en slags visuel tinnitus, et par slag
i luften, hvori ingen kan skrive, og hvorfor skulle
man også det, man kan jo nøjes med at fløjte lidt

in the snow you leave tracks until the big black
snowplow comes rumbling and scrapes the road
but you can always try again, until etc., until
spring comes around, and you're largely levitating over
the new grass like dragonflies and hummingbirds,
these have never set their boots in the substance that
is spoken of here; because now you're just some graphic
on the retina, a sort of visual tinnitus, a couple of beats
in the air on which no one can write, and why should
one do that, one can always get by with a little whistling

176

kattene snakker svensk ved sekstiden
hver morgen, den ene vestgötisk, den anden
endda gotlandsk, de fatter ikke, hvorfor det er
så koldt og øde, det er, fordi jeg endnu drømmer,
og rigtigt sprog står op senere her i huset, og vejret
er simpelthen pisseligeglad med os, ikke en mine
fortrækker det, lige netop som visse mennesker,
pissekolde og svenske, nåja, små slag, min herre,
strindberg har ikke levet forgæves, nej, se, det
er jeg egentlig klar over, hvor tidligt det end er

the cats speak in swedish at around seven o'clock
each morning, the one in visogothish, the other
in gothlandish, they don't understand why it is
so cold and desolate, it's because I'm still dreaming,
and proper languages get up later in this house,
and the weather simply doesn't give a shit, it
doesn't even pretend to, just like certain people,
damned cold and swedish, well, easy now friend,
strindberg did not live in vain, no, see, that much
is finally clear to me, though it is still early

en uhørlig musik bag den hørlige,
så tænker du: aha, et sprog i sproget,
et ansigt i et ansigt, og jeg: ikke i, men
bag noget er der noget, som kat bag træ

an inaudible music behind the audible,
so you think, ah, a language inside language,
a face inside a face, and I: not in it, but behind
something there is something, like a cat behind a tree

det lyner og tordner over den smeltende sne,
nattens dyr skuler under buske og skrammel,
regnen pisker panisk mod taget, vi har stadig
elektricitet, det er nyttigt, men hvem ved hvor
længe, og hvor det var, jeg ville gå hen, inden
alt brød ud, ved ingen; mit øre synger af sig selv

it's thundering and lightning over the melting snow,
night's animals scowl from bushes and junk piles,
rain whips the roof into a panic, we still have
electricity, that helps, but who knows for how long,
or where it was I was meaning to go, before it all
broke loose, no one knows; my ear sings on its own

ja jeg ved jo ikke hvad du tænker på men
hvad med en enkelt lille tanke i retning af
mig og det der sker lige nu lige her og lige
om lidt, vel, det er bare et forslag, lige dér
hvor du selv er, så vidt jeg ved, eller tror,
mens jeg står og venter på en rusten bus?

yes true I don't know what you're thinking but
how about one little thought in the direction of
me and what's happening right here right now and in
a while, well, it's only a suggestion, towards where
you yourself are, as far as I know, or believe,
while I stand here waiting for a rusty bus?

når noget betyder noget, må man være taknemmelig
og også barmhjertig og gå det i møde med armene strakt
til begge sider og håndfladerne vendt mod det kommende,
hvordan det end tager sig ud og lyder, smager og så videre,
for det er en gave, enten fra tingene selv, fra menneskene
inkl. kollegerne eller fra en ven: en sådan betyder sig selv

when something means something, you should be grateful
and also charitable and greet it with your arms outstretched
and your palms open and held out for whatever is coming,
regardless of how it looks and sounds or tastes and so on
because it's a gift, either from things as such, from people
including colleagues, or from a friend: one who means
himself

en død mand sidder over for mig
med øjnene åbne, og solen går ned,
det blodige lys rammer mit ansigt,
jeg kan til sidst ikke se noget som
helst, og det kan han heller ikke

a dead man sits across from me
eyes open, and the sun goes down,
the blood-red light hits my face,
until finally I can't see anything
at all, and neither can he

det levende lever, og vi, vi hænger på
som tyndere øl, det tykke er rigtig spil-
levende, det spræller ud til begge sider,
skummet ejakulerer med pondus, med
vildskab og overbevisning, men uden
dybere omtanke, dets ringe alder bør
huskes, og dog, det tyndere tænker ikke
tættere tanker, det sukker bare og sænker
hovedet som en alt for såret tyr, der ved,
at den snart vil hænge og dryppe fra spid

the lively ones live, and we, we hang
on like thinner beer, the stout is brim-
ful of life, it washes over the sides,
ejaculating foam with force, with wildness
and commitment, but without very much
thought, consider though its youth and in-
experience, and the thinner doesn't think
any denser thoughts, it just sighs and lowers
its head like a far too wounded bull that knows
it will soon hang and drip from a spit

efter dagens indtagelse af blodigt lasede fugle
døser kattene med højst et enkelt øje vågende
over skumring og puslende civilisation, livets
såkaldte mening finder sted hver aften, mens
solsystemet skramler med planeterne, og folk
heromkring saver brænde, græder over spildt
mælk og kærlighed, ærgrer sig ihjel eller bare
spiller skak I garagen, mens mørket fryser til

after the day's fill of bloodied and battered birds
the cats sleep with at most a single eye open
to the dusk and puttering civilization, life's
so-called meaning coming up every night while
the solar system rattles along with its planets, and
people around here cut firewood, cry over spilled
milk and love, annoy themselves to death or just play
chess in the garage while the darkness freezes over

TOSHIYA KAMEI, TRANSLATOR

"The Long Gray Skirt"
by Naoko Awa

I was eight, and my brother Osamu was four. With his hands cupped around his mouth, Osamu imitated a cuckoo's call as he walked ahead of me. The sunlight filtering through the trees flickered on his white cap.

"Coo, coo." Osamu sounded like a pigeon rather than a cuckoo. A real cuckoo cried mysteriously deep inside the forest.

Our father was fishing upstream in the valley. "Don't go far, stay close," he told us many times, but we didn't listen. I still wonder why we went down the river that day.

The river babbled. Dayflowers blossomed at the water's edge. The purple flowers looked like small lamps, continuing endlessly along the river.

Our father had never taken us to the mountain before. We were excited to see rare creatures for the first time— squirrels scurrying up the trunks, incredibly large swallowtail butterflies, red wild strawberries, and small snakes sticking their heads out of bushes. Everything was alive.

"Look, a woodpecker!"

"Do you see that squirrel?"

We cheered every time we saw something new. Even though he was little, Osamu knew the names of many animals. When I taught him the names of flowers, soon he learned them by heart. He was able to recognize thistles, lilies, and bellflowers.

My brother disappeared into the green forest before my eyes, like a swallowtail. I still don't understand how this happened.

"Coo, coo." Osamu's voice faded, and I heard someone scream. When I stopped picking dayflowers and looked up, I saw my brother's cap floating down the stream. He chased his cap, shouting.

"Osamu!" I ran after him. But I wasn't able to catch up. How could a boy of four run so fast? He kept running like a ball rolling down a hill. As the path bent around the river, he disappeared behind the bush. When I came around the bend, he was nowhere in sight. A hayfield spread out as far as the eye could see. Above my head, a lone cloud floated in the sky.

"Osamu!" I called, but I heard nothing but the babbling of the river. My heart beating fast, I stood still for a while.

Suddenly, a nearby bush swayed. "He must be hiding there," I thought. When we walked together, he often hid behind a mailbox or a utility pole to ambush me. Crouched, he would be smothering his laughter until I found him.

"Come out, Osamu!" I cried toward the bush. "Your cap has been washed away," I said. "What are you doing there, Osamu?"

But there was no answer. My voice alone echoed like a strange bird's cry.

The sun hid behind the cloud. The bright green surrounding me darkened, and the mist began to rise.

"Coo, coo!" I heard Osamu's cry in the distance. I felt delighted and cried, "I hate you, Osamu!" Then I held my breath.

In the distance stood a strange woman in a long gray skirt. She was incredibly tall, as tall as a large oak tree. With her arms spread out, she stood like a mother waiting to embrace her child.

Her gray skirt was made of cotton and had many layers. "Coo, coo!" Osamu's cry came from behind the skirt.

186

"A kidnapper!" I thought. I knew the woman had kidnapped Osamu. Come to think of it, I had seen someone like her before. It was when our mother took us to a supermarket. Back then Osamu was still a baby in a carriage. When Mother left us to buy something, a woman crouched and stroked Osamu's head, saying, "What a pretty boy!" She was tall. What was the color of her skirt? Maybe it was gray. Then I burst into tears. Fear ran through my body. As I wailed like an ambulance, my mother came running. The woman left as if she were fleeing.

After that incident, I lived in constant fear of kidnapping. I started to believe the kidnapper would come for children playing outside after dark. I imagined her growing in size. In my mind's eye, she was no longer human. As a large shadow, she wrapped children in a large cloth and took them away.

That day I finally came to face to face with the kidnapper. Maybe she had been after Osamu for a long time. Now he was her captive.

"Osamu," I called. "Come here. Hurry!"

"Coo, coo!" Osamu cried from behind the gray skirt.

"What are you doing?" I tried to run to Osamu, but I became rooted to the spot. "I may get caught, too," I thought. "I should go back and find my father." I took a few steps back.

"Come here," said the kidnapper, waving to me. Her voice was like the roar of wind.

"Where is my brother?" I demanded, my arms crossed behind me. "You took him away. What are you going to do with him?" I asked, turning pale. "Are you going to sell him to a circus?"

The kidnapper laughed silently. Her vine-like bundled hair swayed in the wind. "We have a circus here," she said. "Look." From the pleats of her skirt, she pulled out a pony, a trapeze, and a clown. She made them move as if they were puppets. The pony galloped around. The trapeze swung back and forth like a pendulum. The clown in a baggy black and red suit stuck his tongue out. An accordion played in the background. Applause, cheer, laughter, and whistles mixed together.

My heart beat fast. "It's a circus!" I felt excited and began to run. I ran toward the gray long skirt. But the woman was further away than I had imagined. She stood like a tree in the distance.

I ran and ran, finally reaching the hem of her gray skirt. The woman was a giantess. The horse that looked like a pony was normal in size, and the clown was much taller than I was.

"Miss, would you like to ride the horse?" the clown asked. When I nodded and ran toward the horse, it hid inside the skirt pleat. The clown hurried after the horse. Then the singing, applause, and whistling disappeared into the skirt.

The circus was over, and the silence returned. Osamu's cry faintly drifted from behind the skirt, mixed with the wail of the accordion.

"Osamu!" I cried and ran toward the skirt pleat that swallowed the circus. But the skirt twirled slightly, and another pleat opened before me. "Coo, coo!" Osamu's cry echoed from inside.

Fearfully, I stared into the second pleat. There, spread out before me, was a snow-covered landscape. Flakes of snow fluttered, gradually covering the mountains.

"Osamu, what are you doing there?" I sighed, as if Osamu had done some terrible mischief. "No wonder I can't find you," I murmured and stepped into the snow.

The snow lay deep on the ground. The wind in the distant firs roared like thunder. Maybe Osamu was hiding behind one of the trees, I thought. Maybe he stayed in the shadow of a snow chunk. When I went closer, he would surprise me. I went around and cried, "I found you, Osamu!" But my voice just faded into the flurry of snow. My brother was nowhere in sight. Only his cry was heard in the distance.

I lost track of how long I had been walking. When I realized it, I found a large house in front of me. Under the snow-covered grass roof, I saw a *shoji* window. I heard Osamu's laughter from inside. He laughed cheerfully as if someone were giving him a piggyback ride. Relieved, I called, "Osamu!"

Then the *shoji* window slid open. "Who are you?" said a voice. For a moment my heart froze with fear. There stood a brown bear—large enough to frighten anyone. He carried a baby bear on his back. The baby bear was the one who was laughing earlier. The father bear twitched his ears and demanded, "What do you want?" He measured me with his beady eyes.

"Father, let's have her for dessert," the baby bear said in Osamu's voice, from his father's back.

The father bear nodded. "Yes, she'd make a good dessert."

Becoming pale, I turned and began to run. I don't remember which way I ran. "I'm going to be eaten!" I screamed inside my head. I felt a large dark beast following me close behind, his open jaws closing on my neck. I ran and ran.

When I realized it, I sat by the long gray skirt. As I tried to catch my breath, the skirt twirled again and showed another pleat.

Osamu's voice resonated from inside, like a distant echo. But I couldn't muster enough courage to go inside again. The kidnapper was playing with me. She must have been laughing at me.

I looked up to see her face, but I couldn't see anything. She was too tall.

I was scared. If I kept following my brother, she would make me disappear, too, I thought. "I can't find Osamu. Mother! Mother!" Sobbing, I staggered around the gray skirt.

Each pleat of the gray skirt revealed a distinct world. One pleat showed red mountain lilies in bloom. The next one was an autumn landscape, a field of *susuki* swaying in the wind. "Where are you, Osamu?" I murmured and fearfully peeked into each pleat.

A blue lake lay in one pleat. A boat bobbed on the water, and a forest swayed in the distance. The next one showed a cherry forest. A tunnel of pale pink flowers continued endlessly. Inside, a horse was eating cherry petals. The next one was total darkness. I couldn't see anything, but I heard Osamu's cry: "Coo!" His voice was close and clear. If I reached out my hand, I thought I could touch him. I put one hand inside the pleat and cried, "Osamu!"

Then a blue light flickered in the dark. "A firefly," I thought. Another blue light flickered, and they multiplied like stars.

Suddenly, I felt happy. I went into the pleat and sang, "Ho, ho, fireflies." I heard the river running like ice. I listened intently in the dark and tried to find out where exactly the river was.

Then I realized the blue lights were not fireflies, but day-flowers. What I saw was the blue of dayflowers. In the dark, the flowers shone blue, forming blue signposts along the river. I groped in the dark for Osamu, as if blindfolded.

"Osamu! Osamu!" I kept walking toward Osamu's voice. No matter how far I went, I couldn't touch him. Soon his voice was erased by the babble of the water, and I lost him completely.

Lost in the dark, I didn't know what to do, too tired to keep walking. I was about to collapse. Hugging my knees, I crouched down in the grass, like an abandoned baby rabbit. But in a time like this, it was easier to be a rabbit than to be a human. "If I were a rabbit, I'd be able to sleep in the dark." I thought I would turn into a rabbit and sleep there that night. I decided to look for Osamu in the morning.

"Osamu must be sleeping, too," I thought. "He may have become a rabbit. He may be sleeping in the grass." I closed my eyes.

Then an idea came to my mind. "Don't sleep!" a voice inside me screamed. I opened my eyes and got to my feet. People fell asleep in the mountain and never woke up. "I can't sleep now," I thought. "I'm tired and hungry, but I can't sleep."

My father had told me people would drink coffee or tap each other's shoulder to stay awake. But I was alone. I didn't have anyone who would make me coffee or tap my shoulder to keep me awake. The only thing I could do was . . . to sing.

I began to sing songs I had learned in school. Then I sang songs from way back, TV show songs, every song I knew, even ones I had made up.

These songs kept me alive. The fire dies out, if you don't throw wood into it. I would die, too, when I ran out of songs. While I sang, I looked for the next song, like looking for wood to feed the fire.

After singing for a long time, I noticed something strange. Someone else was singing with me. It was a man's voice. He knew all the songs I knew. He even knew the words to the songs I had made up. Stunned, I stopped singing and cried, "Who are you?"

"Do you want coffee?" the voice asked.

I didn't answer.

"Do you want hot milk instead?"

"Who are you? Where are you?" I asked.

"Only twenty steps ahead of you," the voice answered in a singsong.

I took twenty steps toward the voice.

Then it was light again. A triangular tent appeared before my eyes. The clown stuck his head out of the entrance. He wore a pointy hat and a baggy red and black suit. He said, "Hi."

"Oh, it's you, Mr. Clown!" I cried. "Oh, the circus is here?" As I imagined the whole circus inside this small tent, I felt excited.

But the clown shook his head. "They're all gone. I'm alone," he said. "The horse ran wild and left. I'm waiting for him to come back."

"The horse?" I had seen him in a cheery forest. "I saw him eating cherry blossoms," I said.

"In a cherry forest? Well, I'm relieved," said the clown, blinking. "He'll calm down and come back soon. He loves cherry blossoms. He likes to gallop through falling blossoms. After spring is over, he misses cherry blossoms so much he sometimes goes wild. But the mountain is a mysterious place. If you keep thinking about cherry blossoms, a cherry forest will appear in front of you. The horse finally found his own cherry forest. He's enjoying himself."

"Is that so? If that's true, maybe I could find Osamu, too," I said. "I've been thinking about him for a long time." I sat down and sipped the coffee the clown made. It warmed my body and cheered me up.

"Yes, I'm sure you'll find him. Just keep looking. If you don't like the dark, use the lights of dayflowers."

"The lights of dayflowers?" I repeated.

The clown left the tent and began to pick dayflowers. Soon he made a large bouquet. It shone bright blue. "Use this. You'll find the person you're looking for," he said.

Holding the blue bouquet illuminating the path, I walked along the river. Sometimes I cried, "Osamu!"

"Coo, coo." I heard my brother's call.

"Hey! Osamu!" I cried and brandished the bouquet. Then something flew toward the blue ring of light. It was, without a doubt, the one who was cooing. But it wasn't Osamu. It was a pigeon. I picked it up and stroked its wings, my heart pounding.

The pigeon's breast was warm. I held it in my arms and burst out crying. Tears kept flooding my eyes.

"Oh, she turned my brother into a pigeon!" I thought. Because Osamu wasn't good at imitating a cuckoo, the mountain spirit cast a spell on him. When I called his name, the pigeon shook its breast and cooed.

With the pigeon in my arms, I sat by the river, sobbing. I cried myself to sleep.

My father tells me that I, too, would have died in the mountain if I had slept longer. "What do you mean?" Every time he says this, I shake my head. "Osamu is still alive!" I cry and tell him what happened.

I still believe Osamu became a pigeon, and that he's trapped inside the long gray skirt. But no one believes me. Everyone says my brother drowned in the river, and that his white cap was found floating downstream.

"But when Osamu disappeared, he wasn't wearing his cap," I insist. "He dropped it in the river. While he was chasing it along the water, a woman in a gray skirt kidnapped him. She cast a spell on him and turned him into a pigeon. He's still cooing inside the skirt."

But no one understands me. "You wandered through the mountain for twenty-four hours. You must have imagined things," says my father. "You mistook a large dead tree for a gray skirt." While stroking my hair, he repeats, "We will never, ever go back there again."

IV. Archival Treasures

Fig. 1. "The Embrace of the Tree." Ca. 1922. Photograph (ca.1940) of stone sculpture. Reproduction courtesy of Special Collections and Archives, Missouri State University.

In her mid-sixties, Rose O'Neill stands by her "Sweet Monster" sculpture, which had been moved from Carabas to her Bonniebrook home in Taney County, Missouri.

As psychologist Carl Jung writes, "The unborn work in the psyche of the artist is a force of nature that achieves its end either with tyrannical might or with the subtle cunning of nature herself, quite regardless of the personal fate of the man [sic] who is its vehicle" (*CW* 15 ¶108). Jung continues:

> The creative urge lives and grows in him like a tree in the earth from which it draws nourishment. We would do well, therefore, to think of the creative process as a living thing planted in the psyche. In the language of analytical psychology this living thing is an autonomous complex. (*CW* 15 ¶108)

196

James S. Baumlin, gemma
Bellhouse, Lanette Cadle, et al.[1]

From Kewpies to Monsters: Archetype, Androgyny, and "Evolution" in the Artwork of Rose O'Neill

I was a maker of toys
That made young children smile,
Haunted by terrible wings
And stern gigantic things
That leaned on my shoulders.

—Rose O'Neill, from her Washington Square
notebook (ca. 1920)

I seemed to have been entranced by the idea of the rise of man from animal origins and was always drawing low-slanted beings that pointed behind us. These beings charmed me. . . . We called these drawings "the monsters." . . . People used to wonder how the hand that made the Kewpies could bring forth those monstrous shapes with their mysterious whisperings of natural forces and eons of developing time.

—Rose O'Neill, *Story* (120)

---

[1] Under Missouri State archivist Anne Baker's direction, students from Baumlin's Spring 2010 Honors Writing course took on the task of scanning, describing, and indexing O'Neill's 1920s correspondence and notebooks—over 700 discrete items, comprising six CDs. Were there sufficient space in the by-line above, we would happily include their names, since they provided raw materials for this essay: Thomas R. Barttels, Alison M. Bickers, Joshua L. Campbell, Ashley C. Dameron, Jordyn E. Ewbank, Aaron L. Hinckley, Naomi Kis, Janna M. Kujawa, Victor I. Pierce, Elizabeth A. Propst, Kristen M. Riffle, Marie K. Riti, Sarah A. Rocha, Kayla A. Seiber, Chad W. Sprague, Philip L. Starostka, Justine A. Stewart, and Michelle A. Williams. Of these student-scholars, Ms. Propst deserves special mention, as she served as project "whip" and supervisor, keeping charge over the database.

Fig. 2. "Besieging the Lips of Earth." Ca. 1915-1920. Ink drawing first shown in Paris. Reproduction courtesy of Jimmie Allen.

Man reaches upward as Earth, seemingly hewn from living rock, bends to receive his tribute. Earth's swept-back hair is feminine, though other features remain neutral or androgynous. The image presents an allegory of opposites conjoined by a kiss: of form with matter, humanity with nature, masculine with feminine.

"To be a whole person," writes the post-Jungian feminist Ann Belford Ulanov, "we must come to terms with our own physical, sexual identity and with all those psychic factors which are represented to us by means of the masculine-feminine polarity. Without wrestling with this task of differentiation, . . . we miss the spiritual significance of physical sexuality" (147).

Beginning in the Middle

> All of Miss O'Neill's work is born of an imagination rich in
> fable and mythology, yet free in her personal interpretation
> that makes cloven-hoofed Nature relent in the tender
> expression of a woman's face.
>   —Edythe H. Brown, "Rose O'Neill's Sculptured Drawings" (65)

We begin in March 1922, with Rose O'Neill (1874–1944)
at the height of her powers. The millionaire inventor of
the Kewpie had grown in celebrity, keeping homes in New
York's Washington Square; in Westport, Connecticut; in the
Missouri Ozarks; and on the Isle of Capri. Triumphant from
her Paris showing of the previous year, she had just opened
an exhibition in New York, which would run through most
of that month; and she looked forward to the publication
of her poems, forthcoming later that year from Knopf. The
forty-eight-year-old Rose had, indeed, reached the height of
her wealth, fame, and artistry.

And yet, interviewed by Edythe H. Brown, O'Neill expressed diffidence in showing her serious artwork. "From
a long practice of hiding what I was loving most to make,
I had grown extremely shy" (62), she told the American art
critic, adding, "I must confess that I dreaded 'exposure'"
(64).[2] Punningly, the "exposure" to which she refers was the
*Exposition d'œuvres de Rose O'Neill, du 31 Mars au 14 Avril 1921
inclus*, the Paris exhibition of her work at the Galerie Devambez.

---

[2] An anonymous typescript (likely transcribed from a New York newspaper) reflects similar sentiments:

> While she has been creating Kewpies in all bewitching forms and sizes,
> she has guarded this secret of intensely serious work for her own pri-
> vate delight; but now, Miss O'Neill has yielded to the persuasions [and]
> threats of her friends, who have even suggested that she was cheating
> the world of art. So, last year, the drawings were reluctantly drawn
> from their seclusion and placed on exhibition at the Galerie Devam-
> bez, Paris. And Paris was enthused. . . .

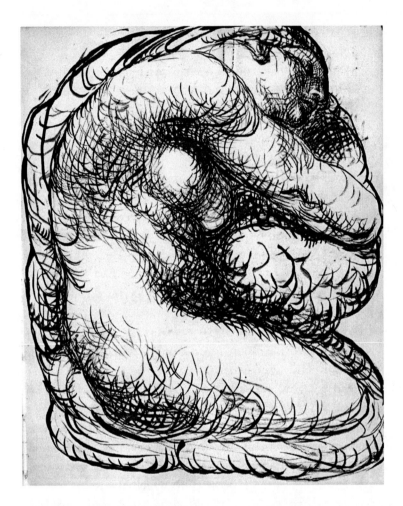

Fig. 3. ["Cradled by Earth"]. Ca. 1925. Ink drawing from the second Carabas "Faun-Book." Reproduction courtesy of Special Collections and Archives, Missouri State University.

The drawing seems a variation on "Man and the Earth" (ca. 1920), first shown in New York.

"I do not love Form less for its expression of Idea," says O'Neill. "It thrills me more vigorously, as the staggering beauty of a mountain or the sea is more piercing for the notions it excites in the human mind" (Brown 68).

A copy of the exhibition catalog survives, in which the French art critic, Arsène Alexandre, offers an appreciative review:

> Madame Rose O'Neill has realized in herself an alliance of paganism with a spiritual conception which the pagan world was unable to formulate. Her drawings are at once somber and full of light, exalted and terrifying. If she owes in a certain measure to Hellenism (a Hellenism modified by ardent modern culture), she owes more to Pan than to Apollo.
>
> And this indeed is very well, for Pan is a more universal god on the whole, and more vital.[3]

Alexandre ends by naming her drawings "poems of earth," works that express "the ascension from matter to the unknown."

Like Alexandre, Brown too found poetry in the art: "Perhaps these extraordinary drawings," writes Brown, "can be best compared to allegorical poetry. What the poet feels in word imagery, Miss O'Neill feels in form. The Idea behind the shape is of equal importance with the witchery of lines and limbs. But this strange artist has also the power upon words. Her poetry is as remarkable as her art."[4] Given their monumental shapes and strong brush strokes, Brown

---

[3] In the next year, O'Neill showed her work in New York City's Wildenstein Galleries. The New York exhibition catalog included a translation of Alexandre's review, which we have followed here. In *Rose O'Neill's Sweet Monsters*, Kirdendall and Haas reprint facsimiles of both catalogs, along with much of the artwork exhibited. (For unnamed works, we have supplied our own titles [in brackets].)

[4] Brown refers to the forthcoming *Master-Mistress* (1922), which scattered "Sweet Monster" drawings among its poetry. Reviewing this collection, the 23 December *Boston Transcript* was extravagant in its praise: "These poems and these drawings make us feel that there is something stupendous about Rose O'Neill. She is not to be judged by any of our ordinary standards. She has in truth outsoared our time and revealed herself as belonging to that small band to whom we willingly accord the title of Master."

Fig. 4. "Consciousness." Ca. 1915-1920. Ink drawing first shown in New York. Reproduction courtesy of Jimmie Allen.

The figure presents a complex allegory, in which "Consciousness" rises out of a maelstrom, separating the cloven-hoofed woman-satyr on the left from a (male) human figure on the right. (Perhaps consciousness is the cause of their torment—that is, of the human creature's separation from instinctual Nature.)

"There are some who have found my pictures revolting," says O'Neill. "They hurt the eye. But I am in love with magic and monsters and the drama of form emerging from the formless" (Brown 67–68).

terms them "sculptured drawings." For their uncannily pre-human/subhuman/superhuman subjects, Rose herself calls them "Sweet Monsters." By whatever name, they pleased . . . and puzzled viewers.

The debate over influences had begun. Reporting on the Galerie Devambez showing, the 1921 Paris *Figaro*[5] called O'Neill "a strange and superb visionary, a rare poet whose work, moving and startling, derives naturally enough from the land of Edgar Alan Poe." Her drawings show "a power-ful conception of natural forces, of untrammeled nature, of the aspirations of the material universe and of its relation to the spirit of life." They are "modeled as by a master sculp-tor," adds the *Figaro*, one who presents "visions (sometimes disturbing) of the monster painfully emerging from mother earth."

The American Brown gives a list of her own: "Some said her drawings were like Poe or Whitman, or the sculp-ture of the Greeks. Some found philosophies in them; and some found sinister terror. Again some said it was not the province of Art to carry so much Idea, if indeed any" (64). Against this last point, O'Neill raised a firm objection. "I do not love Form less for its expression of Idea," she answered: "It thrills me more vigorously, as the staggering beauty of a mountain or the sea is more piercing for the notions it ex-cites in the human mind" (64).

Through the following, it is the "allegory" or *Idea* of O'Neill's "Sweet Monsters" that holds our attention. In a previous essay,[6] we explored the sexual politics of Rose's magazine illustrations and poster art, focusing on her femi-nist commitments as a "modern" woman and suffragette. We focused on the conscious *construction* of womanhood in

---

[5] The *Figaro* review is taken from an anonymous typescript in David O'Neill's possession.

[6] See James S. Baumlin and Lanette Cadle, "Portraits of Womanhood in the Art-work of Rose O'Neill."

Fig. 5. "Images of the Mind." 1912. Pencil drawing. Reproduction courtesy of Jimmie Allen.

Among other possibilities, the drawing presents an allegory on artistic inspiration. A swirl of images (conscious and unconscious) surrounds the woman, shown in a reverie.

"The autonomy of the collective unconscious," writes Jung, "expresses itself in the figures of anima and animus. They personify those of its contents which, when withdrawn from projection, can then be integrated into consciousness" (*CW* 9.2 ¶40).

her artwork of the 1900s, 1910s, and 1930s. During these years, the 1910s especially, Rose sought to re-envision women's roles (and manners and dress codes); empowering her fellows, she sought to give women *a voice*, both in public (through suffrage) and in the home. Through these decades, her feminist commitments followed two broad paths. On the one hand, she drew larger-than-life women, creating heroic/charismatic images; on the other hand, she drew with camera-like realism, depicting women *as they really were* (or wished to be seen), and not *as men* imagined, desired, or sought to possess them. The work of these decades belongs to a single, coherent, conscious social, political, intellectual, artistic enterprise.

But we deferred discussion of her work from the 1920s, as it did not fit neatly within these categories. The work of this, O'Neill's most pregnant artistic decade, re-envisioned not the sociology so much as the *mythology* of woman. Like the great Romantic visionaries who preceded her, Rose intuited that real social change required a reimagining of the human creature—which, for O'Neill, entailed an old/new psychology grounded in androgyny. [7] The literary/artistic vocabulary for this psychology came more or less ready-made in classical pantheism, to which she added the "modernist" insight of Darwinian evolution.[8]

---

[7] Carlin T. Kindelien describes her "kinship to the sensuous semireligious visionary art of William Blake" (651), a precedence that Brown, too, notes: "Miss O'Neill has drawn her inspiration from such an equally living fount of symbolism and allegory as . . . Blake's" (68).

[8] Previous scholarship has noted these several themes. "The challenge that O'Neill presented to the traditional order," writes Miriam Formanek-Brunell, "was not only in her portrayal of women of all ages, but also in her representation of androgyny" (*Story* 17). Formanek-Brunell continues: "In her serious work, O'Neill often dissolved the borders between those qualities typically associated with men and those used to characterize women. . . . In O'Neill's Sweet Monster series . . . she fused neoclassical themes, pagan myths, mystical subject matter, and Darwinian theory to address the issue of gender as a cultural construct" (*Story* 17).

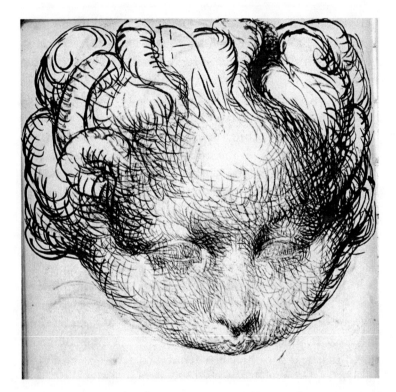

Fig. 6. ["Satyr-Woman"]. Ca. 1925. Ink drawing from the second Carabas "Faun-Book." Reproduction courtesy of Special Collections and Archives, Missouri State University.

The image seems a variation on "Fugitive 13," first shown in New York.

In O'Neill's novel, Garda (1929), the Norwegian artist Thormod prepares to sculpt her bust: studying Garda's face, he "had not failed to observe the little horny lift of the hair at the temples. Perhaps this singularity was caused by a slight perversity of growth, commonly called a 'cowlick.' It may have been that Garda's temples had two 'cowlicks,' and these gave her her little horns. Above each ear was a winged sweep (*Garda* 72). "Satyr-Woman" thus hints at the facial features that Garda would possess in full.

206

It's time to state our thesis, which proceeds in stages. Through the 1920s, Rose turned from poster-making to myth-making, using poetry, fiction, sculpture, and fine art as her media. Anthropomorphizing Nature, she sought to re-describe the human creature as a fertile union-of-opposites, in which a (masculine) psyche finds its habitation and nurturance in a (feminine) earth-body; conjoined, the body and spirit evolve over the millennia. Her "Sweet Monster" drawings appear sculpted, as if carved from rock. In this respect, O'Neill's medium reflects her message: the human creature's origins remain chthonic, raised up out of the living rock of Mother Earth, from which titanic goddess-women spring, giving nurturance to the (male) human psyche, small in comparison but destined to evolve. At the same time, O'Neill celebrates our animal-nature: satyrs, stags, and fauns fill her imagination.

Having mentioned the artist's imagination, we are left to describe the *process* by which O'Neill fashioned her work of the 1920s. We have said that her previous decades' work was "single, coherent, conscious" in conception and execution. Her work of the Twenties was no less coherent and singular in focus; but, time and again through her memoir and notebooks, she asserts the *autonomous, unconscious* origins of her "Sweet Monster" art—as if the mythic images conceived her, and not *vice versa.* [9]

---

[9] We mention the private notebooks, as they provide much of the unpublished material presented herein. We draw from four in particular: her Bonniebrook notebook (begun ca. 1915), in which Rose is already envisioning her "Sweet Monster" art; her Washington Square notebook (begun ca. 1918), whose poetry turns to "Master-Mistress" themes; her first Carabas "Faun-Book" (1922), which explores pantheism (among other subjects); and her second Carabas "Faun-Book" (1925), which tells of her European travels and of the writing of her novel, *Garda.* All these notebooks contain travelogue- and diary-entries, scattering poems and sketches among records of witty conversation. The materials in these notebooks both supplement and complicate O'Neill's "official" autobiography, *The Story of Rose O'Neill,* as edited by Miriam Formanek-Brunell.

Fig. 7. ["Satyr-Man"]. Ca. 1915. Ink drawing from the Bonniebrook notebook. Reproduction courtesy of Special Collections and Archives, Missouri State University.

The image seems a study for "Fugitive 3," first shown in New York. It also seems to prefigure Rose's rendering of Mr. Greenlaw, the satyr-hero of Haniel Long's story, "Professor of Dreams" (1922).

"The collective unconscious contains the whole spiritual heritage of mankind's evolution, born anew in the brain structure of every individual" (*CW* 8 ¶342): so writes Jung in his essay, "The Structure of the Psyche" (1928). He elaborates:

> The collective unconscious—so far as we can say anything about it at all—appears to consist of mythological motifs or primordial images, for which reason the myths of all nations are its real exponents. In fact, the whole of mythology could be taken as a sort of projection of the collective unconscious. . . . We can therefore study the collective unconscious in two ways, either in mythology or in the analysis of the individual. (*CW* 8 ¶325)

208

Her Washington Square notebook, for example, includes an unpublished epigram, "I was the master and the tool":

I was a vendor of toys
That I carved from a clod
But on my shaken shoulder
Staggered the Theban god.[10]

Dionysus—"the "Theban god" of wine, ecstasy and the unconscious—presses down upon the artist, who seems to deprecate her Kewpie-work. As a mere "vendor of toys," she remains her own "master" (as the poem's title suggests); but, when pressed into the pagan god's service, she turns from art's "master" to its "tool"—all of which leads us to the psychology underlying her mature artistry: for it is in the realm of psychology that human sexuality (and sexual identity) and artistic creativity meet.

In illustrating this essay, we have drawn from Rose's private notebooks, as well as from among the artist's studies and sketches; publishing several of these for the first time, we shall present facets of O'Neill's artistry that have lain unexamined. But, before turning to the "allegory" of her mature art, we give a brief summary-analysis of Rose's major work of the late 1920s, a "Celtic" tale illustrating the many themes we have described thus far. We have just called her novel, *Garda*, a "major work," and yet it, too, has languished unstudied, as good as forgotten.

An Interlude on *Garda* (1929)

"Garda" is opulent, with a voluptuous, yearning quality like the music of Tristan. It is wise, sometimes daintily blasphemous, with a compassionate wit.

— From the 24 March 1929 *New York Herald Tribune*

---

[10] The poem-epigraph at the beginning of this essay is a companion piece to this, written on the page opposite.

Fig. 8. ["Garda and Narcissus"]. 1929. Dust jacket illustration. Reproduction courtesy of Special Collections and Archives, Missouri State University.

The brother and sister are figured, with an oak- or acanthus-leafed ram's head to the right. We have quoted the 24 March 1929 *New York Herald Tribune*, which calls *Garda* "opulent, with a voluptuous, yearning quality . . . . It is wise, sometimes daintily blasphemous, with a compassionate wit." Shall we name its "blasphemous" themes? Necromancy, reincarnation, paganism, voyeurism, forbidden desire (both homoerotic and incestuous, though unconsummated in either case), abandonment of marriage, murder, suicide: quite enough for one novel.

There were other, more mixed reviews. "Over the book hangs the faery beauty that is the Irish gift to art," writes the 20 April *New York Evening Post*. It is "that nebulous beauty," the *Post* reviewer continues, "entrancing, remote, *and unreal*" (emphasis added). The 5 May *New York Times* writes, "In less skilled hands the story at times would border on the grotesque because of its bizarrerie, but with Miss O'Neill it remains lyrically beautiful." And the 12 June *New Republic* pulls no punches: "The characters are rich in contrast and weird enough to suit the sharpest craving for the grotesque. The method of revealing the plot in its larger aspects is skillful and competent. What ruins the book is an excessive Celticism in the style. It is completely undisciplined." Though contradictory *in toto*, each is right in its way.

210

Early in the novel, O'Neill's sensuous protagonist lies by the lakeside, drying her hair. Her bathing companions, Starke and Garda's twin brother, Narcissus, dwell upon the sight of her:

> A slight wind passed over her head and ruffled her drying tresses.
> "She's getting all covered with acanthus leaves," said Starke.
> "She's getting all horns like a stag, you mean," added the brother. (*Garda* 57)

More than clothe her in Nature, they transform her into a stag of Artemis, pagan goddess of chastity, fertility, animals, and the hunt. This fusion of naturalist symbolism, of stag and acanthus leaves, finds its way onto the novel's cover art. Later again the narrator describes her bathing:

> She was a perilous sight going about in a bathing costume. Narcissus and Starke looked in her direction as little as possible. . . . When the grandmother once exclaimed: "For heaven's sake, look at those breasts!" [Starke] had replied, *Those* are not breasts, they're weapons. They would stab a man to death." (64)

Of course, O'Neill *wants the reader* to look, even if the men fight temptation. As a "modern" woman of the 1920s, Garda shows more than her ankles. "'Legs, splendid legs!' cried Narcissus" (58), decrying the Victorians for hiding "under petticoats, the walking tents" (58):

> "And now they're out," said Garda.
> "They're unsheathed like swords," he continued.
> "They've never been out like this since Artemis."
> Starke kept his look away from Garda's bright thighs. So did Narcissus. (58)

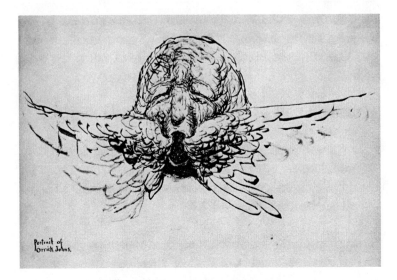

Portrait of
Orrick Johns.

Fig. 10. "Portrait of Orrick Johns." 1926. Ink drawing from the second Carabas "Faun-Book." Reproduction courtesy of Special Collections and Archives, Missouri State University.

O'Neill transforms her friend, American poet and playwright Orrick Johns (1887–1946) into a "Sweet Monster," turning his whiskers into wings. The image seems to cast him as a wind-god, presiding over inspiration and prophecy. Johns, we have suggested, was the "first reader" of *Garda*, and he provided a dust jacket blurb.

As Rose notes in her autobiography, "my circle has always been composed of utterers and I have Boswellized them, writing what they said in my note-books with the utmost exactness. . . . This has gone on for years until the books are full of brilliant bits. A publisher, hearing of them, came to see and said he had never seen anything so dazzling" (*Story* 118–19). Along with Johns, the O'Neill "circle" (as she puts it) included Lebanese poet, Kahlil Gibran (1883–1931), American poet, Clement Wood (1888–1950), American poet and publisher, Haniel Long (1888–1956), and Bengalese poet, Dhan Gopal Mukerji (1890–1936). Rose names others—E. A. Robinson, Max Eastman, Charlotte Perkins Gilman, Arthur Willis Colton, Witter Bynner, Marion Reedy, Gilbert Cannan (*Story* 116–17)—but their writings and influence do not figure in this present study.

212

The Artemis myth here envelopes the two men, who struggle to avoid Actæon's fate: caught gazing upon the naked Artemis bathing, the mythic Actæon is himself transformed into a stag and hunted down by the moon goddess's avenging hounds. Equated with Nature, Garda's sexuality is at once celebrated, intensely desired, *and feared* by the two men who love her—and who love each other. And she loves them both, as well.

It is a strange love-triangle that the sister presides over. The novel opens with Garda returning to the lakeside village of her childhood, having abandoned her second husband, Bastiano: a virile, passionate, possessive Italian. "What kind of face would you say she had?" Starke asks his more-than-friend, Narcissus. (In her absence, the two men had grown close, "discover[ing] it difficult to separate" [18].) "Well, what do you want to discuss?" Narcissus rejoins:

> "Her little chin?" . . . It has a deep cleft in it. . . .
> She's broad between the eyes and she has horns. . . .
> My face is a caricature of hers, and her soul is a caricature of mine. In fact, she has no soul. She is my substance. She robbed me of substance in the womb.
> . . . She lamed me. . . . She grew her beauty on me like a flower on a dunghill. She is my material. I am her soul. We are that perilous pair." (1–2).

A "perilous pair," indeed. Gazing upon his poolside reflection, the mythic Narcissus falls tragically in love with his own reflection. For O'Neill's Narcissus, the man's twin sister—whom he nicknames Narcissa—is fated to become his mirror-image, presenting an equally impossible love.

"A 'damned virgin,' as he called himself" (137), Narcissus was lamed from birth; but while broken physically, he is strong in spirit. O'Neill wishes us to take him at his word, thus, when Narcissus declares that "She is *my material.* I am

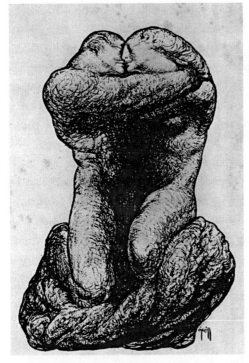

Fig. 9. "The Master-Mistress." Ca. 1920. Ink drawing first shown in New York; also used as a book illustration (1922). Reproduction courtesy of Special Collections and Archives, Missouri State University.

"The letters you write to each other must look like those last fragments of Sappho," declared Clement Wood during one of his Carabas visits. In "Silk" (the first of "Four Poems to Kallista," published in *Master-Mistress*), Rose offers one of her finer lyrics to her sister:

> When all the forge-fires of the day expire,
> I put on you, my love, as silk attire;
> I make me fair with you, my silk, and wear
> The smile you give my lips to make me fair.
> I don you as a garment, deep impearled,
> To lord it in the world; . . . .
> And then, ah then, where is my penury?
> Not mine the ragged heart that is for hire!
> I put on you, my love, as silk attire. (1-6, 10-12)

Reviewing *Master-Mistress* in the 6 December issue of *The Nation*, Wood calls it "one of the significant volumes of American poetry," containing "more than a score of poems of such amazing beauty and strength that they push out the bourn of English singing. To say that she is at once established as a leading poet of America today is less true than untrue. She is as American and as much of today as the wind: and no more. She is a sport, a freak: dateless, eternal."

214

her soul." It is not the scandalous whisper of incest, but the mystical/alchemical longing of soul-for-soul (and of soul-for-body) that O'Neill strives to depict.[11]

Through cronies' gossip, the reader learns of the siblings' intertwined fate. From an Irish wet nurse, an old lady heard it said "that *they had been lovers in another life*" (43; emphasis added). On its dust jacket, the publishers declare *Garda* a "book in the great Celtic tradition." If Celtic, indeed, in its *mythos,* the further gossip gives some proof: "'That strange old woman,' she continued, 'said she had known of other instances—that disembodied lovers, yearning after each other for a long empty time, make the mistake of rushing into the same womb to ease their hearts'" (43). "They *were* one self, imprisoned in separate bodies" (43; emphasis in original), the old lady concludes, and now "*can only yearn without relief*" (44; emphasis added).

And then there is Starke, strong in body but broken in spirit, rendered incapable of loving women by the memory of a horrifying affair that occurred in his teens (and which he keeps secret from Garda). But brother Narcissus has grown to love him, and sister Garda falls in love with him, too. Together, they form a sexually-charged if celibate triangle.

And then there is Bastiano, who comes to retake what is his. "I forbid you to go back to *him*," Starke says, speaking of Bastiano. "Rather than that," Garda replies, "would you take me for yourself and risk my knowing everything?" speaking

---

[11] "She has *no soul*," we have heard Narcissus say, and his declaration—more than metaphor, to his mind—anticipates our later analysis. "Woman has no anima, *no soul*," writes Jung, "but she has an *animus*" (*CW* 17 ¶338). Punning on the Latin etymology (anima=soul), Jung's anima/animus distinction remains archetypal, *not* theological in intent. Still, the distinction holds for O'Neill's *Garda*, whose siblings seem caught up in a mutual anima/animus projection. Subsequent paragraphs will explain; our aim here, simply, is to assert the cultural provenance of the brother's soul-talk. Though an outrage to common sense, his words come *verbatim* from one of the age's preeminent psychologists.

Fig. 11. ["Dr. Greenlaw and Student"]. 1922. Magazine illustration. Reproduction courtesy of Special Collections and Archives, Missouri State University.

An illustration from Haniel Long's "Professor of Dreams"—a modern fairytale, into which O'Neill weaves her pantheistic images. President Burbage, head of an American college, laments the spiritual torpor of students who study business while neglecting the heart's poetry. But a stranger arrives, "introduc[ing] himself as Greenlaw by name, . . . a teacher of the art of dreams" (355). Clearly his name invokes the power (or *law*) of Nature and its hold on the human imagination.

Professing "literature, the world of the passionate mind" (357), Dr. Greenlaw "kindled the imagination" (356) of students, who soon could barely survive others' "lectures on . . . salesmanship" (357). Communing with Nature, they learn its whisperings: one girl in particular "sent her landlady into hysterics by narrating to her . . . what she had heard voices say under her eaves at daybreak" (356).

Yet Dr. Greenlaw searches for that one complete convert. "At dawn there were cloven prints in the soft garden ground beneath my window," he tells his class, "yet I have found no cloven imprint on all you have written" (358). Some days later he receives a letter—from Burbage's son—upon which "was the black imprint of a hoof" (358), followed by poetry. Questioned, young Burbage responds, "If they dance below your window, sir, why cannot they dance across my page?" (358). The student gives proof of the "ancient presences" (359) awakened in him, reciting poems of his metamorphoses—first into a goat, then into a satyr, and then into the night mist.

"You are mad," Dr. Greenlaw declares, "charmingly, evasively mad. I have sown it, the ancient seed" (361). "But enough," he continues, his task completed: "I must go" (361). Jumping out his office window, he disappears into the forest, leaving his disciple in tears. Still, the satyr had brought out a poignant poet from a world of money-making emptiness.

216

of Starke's guilty secret (144; emphasis in original). "Yes," Starke responds,

> "but let's not think of such a hideous alternative. You won't go back to him . . . . You'll go away from this cursed lake with your brother, and wander forever with your soul in perpetual sweet talk. There must be no more division of that. You should never have left him. You're safe there. And he will sublime you again. Good-bye." (144–45)

With *noblesse oblige*, Starke gives up his claims to "the two Narcissans" (217) as O'Neill comes to call brother and sister united. And here "the pencil rises into alchemy," as Rose puts it in her Washington Square notebook: by acknowledging the brother as her "soul," who will in time "sublime" her, Starke invokes an ancient alchemical tradition, one that treats Narcissus/Narcissa as a *mysterium conjunctionis*—an archetypal wedding of sun and moon.[12] (But ironies along with mysteries may cohabit the same text. *Who knows how much Freud O'Neill knew?* Is it a "sublim[ation]" of the Freudian sort that Starke imposes upon Garda, a transformation of incestuous desire into "perpetual sweet talk," rendered sexless precisely by its being "perpetual"? How can we know?)

"And what about you without *us*?" (145; emphasis in original), asks Garda, who "stopped him with the intense vibration of her call" (145). This will not be the last time Starke obeys her "intense" calling, though he pays a price. Given her resolve to stay, Starke vows to watch over her bedroom door.

Of course, nothing keeps the husband from bursting in, confronting her. "Everything was beautiful" at first, Garda admits. "She paused and added: 'I mean, of course, till we

---

[12] "I have drunk the sun, but he has spilled the moon" (52), says Garda of her brother, giving expression to the archetypal imagery.

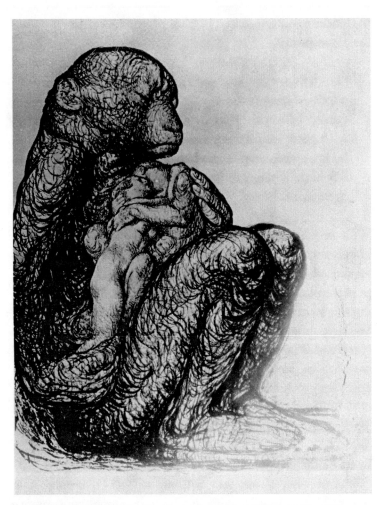

Fig. 12 "The Future in the Lap of the Past." Ca. 1915–1920.
Ink drawing first shown in Paris. Reproduction courtesy of Jimmie
Allen.

On the back of a copy Rose had made of the original, she inscribes the
following poem:

> The Past is dreaming
>   of things to come—
> The more perfect things appearing
>   in the earthy lap.

got too near—until we married'" (160). The notion of getting "too near" another hints at the character's psychology, though the phrase remains ambiguous: for all Garda's sensuality, we are left questioning (in Freudian manner) whether it is sex, or marriage *per se*, that destroys love. Impulsively, Bastiano shoots the protective Starke, leaving him for dead, and then heads to the lake, taking his own life by drowning.

In the final chapter, Starke lies comatose on his deathbed, the physicians having given up hope. "*Garda, Let him go!*" (308; emphasis in original) Narcissus implores: "'Sweet tenacious, cruel substance of life that you are!' he said. 'Release this being. Don't you know that his wounds are too deep for further endurance?'" (300-01). But here, despite (or perhaps in response to) her brother's pleadings, Garda at last reveals her powers. The novel ends:

> And against that persuasion, like a shaft of fierce, indisputable granite in a desert, stood up the determination of Narcissa. She was reiterating a word into that poor deaf ear, the word "Live." His veins throbbed to that reiteration, and the word seemed incapable of ceasing . . . . Then her whisper changed its form to an inquiry which repeated itself with the same fearful persistence.
>
> "Will you live?"
>
> The night was nearly at its end, and the rain had ceased, when there was a tremor down the rigid body . . . . [U]nder that force of strong interrogation, like the voice of a root underground, came up a sepulchral reply. Starke had answered, "Yes."
>
> Narcissus leaped to his feet in horror. He stood a moment staring, then uttered a stifled cry of furious joy and acquiescence; and for the first time the brother and sister kissed. (305)

BLACK MAGIC

Poem & drawings
by Rose O'Neill

Fig. 13 "Black Magic." Ca. 1925. Ink cover-art (unpublished). Reproduction courtesy of Jimmie Allen.

Rose's title-page for a projected collection of poetry and drawings. A playground of anamorphosis, the drawing puts O'Neill's imaginative powers on full display: embedded within are Rose's signature wings, which transform into owls; men and women (and monsters) take partial shape; eyes stare out from all parts of the crowded composition.

"Whoever speaks in primordial images speaks with a thousand voices" (*CW* 15 ¶128), Jung declares, describing "the secret of great art" thus:

> The creative process . . . consists in the unconscious activation of an archetypal image, and in elaborating and shaping this image into the finished work. By giving it shape, the artist translates it into the language of the present, and so makes it possible for us to find our way back to the deepest springs of life. Therein lies the social significance of art: it is constantly at work educating the spirit of the age, conjuring up the forms in which the age is most lacking. The unsatisfied yearning of the artist reaches back to the primordial image in the unconscious which is best fitted to compensate the inadequacy and one-sidedness of the present. The artist seizes on this image, and in raising it from deepest unconsciousness he brings it into relation with conscious values, thereby transforming it until it can be accepted by the minds of his contemporaries according to their powers. (*CW* 15 ¶129)

220

A strange tale, indeed, as Garda calls Starke back from the dead and brother and sister share their first kiss. "Life has no existence without necromance," O'Neill had mused some years earlier, in her Washington Square notebook; Garda puts this *bon mot* to the test.

Writing in 1926 during her summer tour of Italy, Rose shared the manuscript, chapter by chapter, with her entourage. Orrick Johns, as she notes in her autobiography, "had come to Venice in time to read my story *as it came alive*. When I had *Garda* partly done, he said: "You're a she-cloud. That's what you are. It's remarkable writing. It's strange, it's incredible, it's gorgeous, *it's monstrous*. . . . I'm bitten by the scorpions of your pen." (*Story* 136; emphasis added). Here (as elsewhere in her memoir), Rose quotes from her voluminous notebooks—in this case, from the second Carabas "Faun-Book."

Placing the notebook and the "official" memoir side by side, one finds the latter more reticent and occasionally self-censoring. On 11 August 1926, O'Neill read the last chapter (as mentioned above) to Johns. Her "Faun-Book" records his response. "I think you were afraid of the forgiveness of God," said Johns, adding, "you wrote this book to make sure you would not get it." Of course he was being witty, touching lightly on the book's "daintily blasphemous" themes, as one contemporary reviewer put it. Still, Rose had some explaining to do, to her brother Clarence especially.

Whereas O'Neill's *Master-Mistress* (1922) raised eyebrows with its Sapphic poems to her younger sister, Callista, *Garda* upped the ante in exploring the love of brother and sister. It is no wonder that Rose needed to prepare her own Clarence (nicknamed "Clink") for the shock. As she writes in her memoir:

> My youngest brother, Clink, joined me in Venice. I told Clink that I had written *Garda* and put him in

it as Garda's twin brother, Narcissus. "Oh, Clink, I hope I haven't put things in my story that you'll want out when you see it." With a wave of his hand, he said, "Well, publish it first, publish it first. I like to burn my bridges before I come to them." (*Story* 137)

Her "Faun-Book" tells the further story. It turns out that Clink "was a bit shocked" at Narcissus and Narcissa "both loving Starke." "But you see," Rose explained, "both soul and substance must love him. The allegory is complete." She continued: "You see, *they are all made out of our essence*, our Narcissism, Clink. We cannot tell Callista from Garda, me from the grandmother, you from the three, nor Narcissus from the lake" (emphasis added).

If Clink took her explanation in Jungian-archetypal terms, then all was well; if he took it in Freudian terms, then Rose's explanation would seem a smoke screen. At this point, perhaps it is our turn to explain Rose's soul/substance "allegory."

Warring Readings / Warring Psychologies

> Clement Wood: "Only R. O'Neill's gods neigh when they mate."
> Rose: "My gods generate *by yearning*, alone."
> —From O'Neill's second Carabas "Faun-Book"
> (emphasis added)

In Rose O'Neill's lifetime, two schools of depth psychology predominated. Highly popular (if easily vulgarized), Sigmund Freud's psycho-sexual theory interpreted art as a *sublimation* of sexual energy (libido, so-called). Within this model, the conscious work provides a playground for the artist's rationalized, repressed or otherwise "hidden" (being culturally

222

forbidden) fantasies, fears, and desires. Reflecting the artist's "family romance" and the personal traumas accruing therefrom, the Freudianized artwork becomes indistinguishable from neurosis.

It is too easy to Freudianize Rose in this vulgar manner. Her stories come too much from life: her female protagonists typically endure not one but two husbands, in the end abjuring marriage altogether. In place of husbands they long for their soul-mate, often a brother or sister. Though dreaming visionaries, they are stunning beauties whose gendered bodies serve both as sensuous weapons and as the soul's prison. Flaunting conservative social conventions, they live by the High-Romantic values of imagination unfettered, beauty adored, art-as-experience, life-as-mystery. (Plus, they require a daily dose of witty conversation and repartee.)

Through the proceeding analysis, we could not avoid Freudian terms entirely; through the remainder, we shall approach O'Neill's art through the archetypal psychology of Freud's warring-twin rival, Carl Jung. As Jung understood it, the psyche reveals layers deeper than Freud's "personal" unconscious, with its repressed traumas, fears, and forbidden desires. The Jungian "collective" unconscious (from which art flows) precedes personal experience, being no less than the instinctual, "racial memory" of the human species—"the whole history of the race" (*Story* 125), as the Parisian press described Rose's own "Sweet Monster" drawings.

The Jungian archetypes—those varied personifications of the "collective" unconscious, which we meet culturally in myth and individually in our own dreaming—exist independently of/within the psyche. An archetype "speaks to" the artist (such as Rose) in the manner of a *daimon*, in a voice distinctive from her own; often (though not always, as post-Jungian theorists point out), one's inner guidance presents itself in trappings of the opposite sex.[13] (O'Neill's, as we shall see, is a masculine muse.) And the artist who gives her imagination over to the *daimon* discovers that art *comes to* the artist, *chooses* the artist, and not *vice versa*. "On July 19, [1926,] it came upon me suddenly to write my novel *Garda*" (*Story* 136): so writes O'Neill in her memoir, following notes in her second Carabas "Faun-Book." "It had taken me only a few days more than a month to write" (*Story* 136), the ease of which she attributes to the promptings of her muse, "that old fantastical duke of dark corners,"[14] shadowy and playful: "There wasn't any stain of volition about it. No abuse of the will. It was the dear old scoundrel having his fun. My scoundrel. He has not failed me" (*Story* 136). In "Marriage as a Psychological Relationship" (1925)—published the year Rose began her second Carabas "Faun-Book"—Jung writes of the contrasexual archetypes, the anima (within man) and animus (within woman):

> Every man carries within him the eternal image of woman, not the image of this or that particular woman, but a definite feminine image. This image is fundamentally unconscious, an hereditary factor of primordial origin engraved in the living organic system of the man, an imprint or "archetype" of all the ancestral experiences of the female, . . . —in short,

---

[13] As Polly Young-Eisendrath writes, "Jung's contrasexuality is a contribution to depth psychology that problematizes the 'opposite sex,' tracing the shadow of Otherness back to its owner. In contrast to Freud's narrowly focused theories of castration anxiety and penis envy . . . Jung's gender theory is fluid and expansive in its potential uses in a post-modern, decentered world" (224). As a post-Jungian feminist, Young-Eisendrath offers "to save" Jung by reinterpreting the more misogynist aspects of his anima/animus model. (On this point, see also Ulanov.)

[14] Quoting *Measure for Measure* (4.3.163–64), Rose's "fantastical duke of dark corners" invokes the image of Shakespeare's Vincentio, archetypally a master of disguise, who observes and controls affairs from behind the scenes. This passage, too, is taken from the second Carabas "Faun-Book."

an inherited system of psychic adaptation. . . . The
same is true of the woman: she too has her inborn
image of man. (*CW* 17 ¶338)

Elsewhere, Jung elaborates: more than "the deposit ... of all
women's ancestral experiences of man," the animus "is also
a creative and procreative being" (*CW* 7 ¶336), generative of
art. In its positive aspect (the archetypes remain ambivalent
in their influences upon ego-consciousness), the "old fantastical duke" serves as a psychic companion, word-smith inspiration, and worldly guide.[15] Had she known Jung,[16] O'Neill
would have come to an understanding of what is expressed
yearningly, if largely unconsciously, in her art: which is that
successful marriage to another facilitates and reflects an in-
ternal, psychical wedding of ego-consciousness with the archetypal "Other" within.

Before seeking love from others, one must learn to love
self—and all aspects of the Self. Love seeks wholeness, and
wholeness comes through a *conjunctio oppositorum*: a union
of opposites, of form with matter, of flesh with spirit, of
male with female (and, as O'Neill would add, of animal with
human). Of course Rose glimpses love through *projection's*
"Narcissan" mirror,[17] seeking fulfillment through an androgynous union of Self and Other. While from a Freudian standpoint Rose's writing (in *Garda* and *Master-Mistress*)

[15] Much like the mythic Hermes, thus, the mature animus acts as a *psychopomp* (*CW*
9 ¶33), a spiritual "messenger" between the woman artist's ego-consciousness
and her larger Self (again, see Ulanov).

[16] By the mid-1920s, Jung's reputation (among American intellectuals) had been
affirmed: translations had begun to appear, and he gave his first seminar in English in 1925.

[17] For Jung (as for Freud), projection remains a primary mechanism of the human psyche. Regarding the anima/animus within, Jung writes: "since this image
is unconscious, *it is always unconsciously projected upon the person of the beloved*, and is
one of the chief reasons for passionate attraction or aversion" (*CW* 17 ¶338;
emphasis added).

borders on taboo, from a Jungian perspective it expresses that great healing mission of the human spirit, which is to recover our wholeness in a divided world, within our divided, gendered bodies.[18] Rose had become a Jungian, whether she knew it or not.

So much for theory: readers will need to look elsewhere for further primers in archetypal psychology.[19] We trust that our analysis of O'Neill's mature artistry can stand on its own, and we do not mind if readers turn away from the Jungian vocabulary, trading in the term *archetype* for the equally serviceable *myth*. We know that Rose was a student of the imagination, and that she built a coherent aesthetic upon the imagination and its mysteries. We also know that androgyny—the mystic wedding of "brother sun" and "sister moon"—remained an abiding theme of her life's work. Finally, know that Rose *was not alone* in fashioning a pantheistic *mythos* supportive of androgyny. We have mentioned those poets and artists of the O'Neill "circle," who visited (and stayed, often for months at a time) at Carabas and her other haunts; their cross-influences deserve a brief side-glance.

Collaborations

"I have drunk the sun, but he has spilled the moon."
—Rose O'Neill, *Garda* (52)

---

[18] "Jung interpreted incest images . . . not concretely but symbolically, as indicating the need for a new adaptation *more in accord with the instincts*" (Sharp). Such agrees with O'Neill's myth-making, though it "differed so radically from the psychoanalytic view that it led to [Jung's] break with Freud" (Sharp). We should restate that this aspect of our thesis pertains to Rose's *art* solely, and *not* to her biography.

[19] For further discussion, see Sharp; Young-Eisendrath; and essays in Baumlin, Baumlin, and Jensen.

226

We have already quoted the epigraph given above, which Garda speaks in reference to her brother. In fact, Rose had first heard the phrase from Dhan Gopal Mukerji, India's first "modern" poet to achieve international fame. A regular visitor at Carabas, Mukerji was speaking *of Rose* and of her sun-moon relationship with sister Callista. Affirmations of the sisters' two-in-oneness flowed from Mukerji's mystic/poetic imagination, which Rose duly recorded in her notebooks, using them later (and often *verbatim*) in her published writing. We lack space to show this, but several of the more "metaphysical" images in *Garda* come directly from the Bengali's table-talk.

And then there's the Lebanese artist and poet, Kahlil Gibran, with whom Rose is said to have taken lessons in writing.[20] Both had been students in sculpting under Auguste Rodin (1840–1917), and Rose stayed with Gibran while in Paris. The Lebanese poet's vision of spiritual love, which affirms the unity of all things, resonates through Rose's work (Kindelien 651); indeed, his *Sand and Foam: A Book of Aphorisms* (1926)—published while O'Neill was composing *Garda*—so strongly anticipates Rose's androgynous mysticism that one wonders if she kept a copy by. "Every man loves two women," writes Gibran: "the one is the creation of his imagination, and the other is not yet born." In his poetry, thus, the Jungian anima is prefigured. Divided into ego-consciousness and a deeply-layered unconscious, the Jungian Self is also given succinct expression: "MAN IS TWO men," Gibran declares: "one is awake in darkness, the other is asleep in light." Most telling is his recognition of the *self-love* that romantic love awakens: "When I stood a clear mirror before you, you gazed into me and saw your image. / Then you said, 'I love you.' / But in truth you loved yourself in me."

---

[20] And Rose, in turn, presented Gibran with a pencil and water-color portrait; housed in the Smithsonian Museum of American Art, it remains O'Neill's best-known piece of serious artwork.

Finally, there is the Burmese-born and British-educated poet, Haniel Long, best remembered for his short story collection, *Notes for a New Mythology* (1926). Included in this collection is the fairytale-like "Professor of Dreams." First published in the July 1922 *Century Magazine*, Haniel's story was inhabited by satyr-art, being lavishly illustrated by Rose's pen. More than a friendly favor, Rose turned her illustrations into a collaboration between writer and artist over the subject of pantheism. We can go further. Long's book title, *Notes for a New Mythology*, invokes Rose's own artistic enterprise; arguably, the preface to his *Notes* reads as a manifesto for the O'Neill "circle," at least regarding its mythic commitments. "I want to re-possess all the gods I love," Long writes: "I want to see them in the American landscape" (*Notes* 16). He elaborates:

> The gods, the goddesses, the demi-gods, the heroes, titans, and spirits of good and evil are the pageant of eternity. It is far too long a procession to watch the whole of, or to understand in full. We are children, and must soon go home and be put to bed; but what we can see of this procession, let us see. In our starved twentieth-century existence with nothing to look at but machinery, it is a sight which will do us good. And let's not make the mistake of believing that the gods come to us only from the past; if they are real, they come to us from the future as well, and bear in their hearts our destiny. Delicious germs! Let us be alive with them; with them in our world we shall not be lonely. On the contrary, like Thoreau at Walden, we shall have many callers, "especially in the moonlight when nobody calls." (*Notes* 16)

Clearly, Freudian neurosis falls before the very *collectivity* of Rose's mature art. Her writerly "blasphem[ies]," whether

"Celtic" or Hellenic (or "modern") in origin, cannot be reduced to the work of a private imagination. Whether conscious or unconscious, Rose's artistry rests in inspiration, guidance, and partnership.

So we turn at last to the imaginative process underlying O'Neill's mature artwork, where archetypal forces once again come to the fore.

Imagining "Sweet Monsters"

> O Muse Incarnate!
> Speak out to the sunshine
> The Songs of the Ages
> That lie slumbering
> In thy bosom sweet.
>
> —Rose O'Neill, "An Unfinished Song,"
> (dated "Jan 15 1920. 10 p.m.")
> from the Washington Square notebook

O'Neill, as we have seen, was a modern myth-maker who worked with primordial images of archetypal origin and who sought "to solve" the problem of gender-difference (as her culture confronted it, and as we still largely face it today) by recovering the ancient *mysterium conjunctionis*: that sacramental/alchemical union-of-opposites that allows each term to complement and complete and yet differentiate and preserve its Other. The paradox of *alter et idem*, of a "second self" that preserves the "otherness" of the Other in all its mystery, is the great enterprise of O'Neill's mature artistry; and it is best understood, not through its conscious *products*—the individual works of art—but rather through its psychological process, as recorded in drafts, studies, sketches, notebooks: those places where the archetype is first glimpsed raw and half-shaped, prior to its conscious (re-)working as craft.

229

In her autobiography, Rose O'Neill describes the Parisian reception of her "Sweet Monster" art, a series that she had begun drawing a half-decade prior, while living in New York:

> In 1921 I went to Paris and in the winter showed my "monster" drawings at an exhibition at the Devambez Galleries. . . . I was very much surprised at the lovely interest [the exhibitions] created. . . . There was a great variety in the spectators who came. There were workmen in long blouses along with Anatole France, Cocteau, Gertrude Stein, priests, nuns, fashionable women, and army officers in uniform. The newspapers talked a bit about how I had captured in them the whole history of the race. (*Story* 125)

While she describes the exhibition matter-of-factly, her process of invention receives careful attention. Keep in mind that "the Kewpies *were born* in 1911" (*Story* 94; emphasis added): while staying in the Ozarks at Bonniebrook, Rose "had a dream . . . where they were all doing acrobatic pranks on the coverlet" of her bed (*Story* 95). *In a dream*, the Kewpies *came to her*. Whether or not we believe the story, the Kewpies' "birthing" (and, soon after, their mass production into myriad forms: dolls, tableware, candies, car hood ornaments) made Rose fabulously rich.

And, ironically, the success of her Kewpie industry freed her from the drudge-work of magazine illustration to pursue serious art:

> Now that I had plenty of money I did not illustrate as much *but let my hand and imagination have free play*. I would pull up the big rocking chair under the light and let myself go. I am ashamed to be seen when I suffer or when I toil. In the latter case *my consciousness*

has gone away. I leave my cadaver behind . . . . Often I would have no plan before beginning. The plan seemed hidden in the hand itself. *Then satyr-like heads and half-beastly shapes would appear on the paper and the Idea would loom.* (*Story* 120; emphasis added)

Marvelous nights!" she exclaimed, "with the sound of passers in [Washington] Square growing few—perhaps a moon crossing the sky beyond my large high windows and rustling images of ancestral things surging through my head and projecting themselves on paper" (*Story* 120). The effect was intoxicating: "Late in the night I would get out of the 'Drunken Sailor' and, half drunk myself with visions, lay my drawing or drawings (sometimes there would be several) in the portfolio and stagger off to bed. Another monster had been born" (*Story* 120).

Clearly Rose practiced "active imagination" (*CW* 14 ¶706), a Jungian technique of "dreaming with open eyes," as Daryl Sharp puts it ("Jung Lexicon"), giving voice to the archetypes through creative self-expression: that is, through music, dance, writing or (as in O'Neill's nightly exercise) drawing. And the "monsters" *came to her*, just as the Kewpies had done. After an evening's work, she would retire "half drunk . . . with visions."[21] But while we are all artists *in the imagination*, few of us possess the craft capable of translating our imaginings into real art. In her biography, Rose describes her process:

I made these drawings in an intricate network of lines with a small brush and India ink. . . . The web of lines took time. And that was the fun of it. Not to conclude—to go on deliriously sculpting the

---

[21] For "creative power," as Jung writes, "is mightier than its possessor. If it is not so, then it is a feeble thing, and . . . will nourish an endearing talent, but no more" (*CW* 17 ¶206).

form, prolonging the delight. While I drew them, I had ecstatic images of the up-surge of life from the "ancestral slime." This progression seemed to me the epic of epics. (*Story* 120)

It was previously mentioned that the "Sweet Monsters" belong to O'Neill's maturity; in fact, the images first came to her at age twenty, in 1894. Her father had just bought Bonniebrook in Taney County, Missouri, and she describes her first wagon trip from Springfield through the rugged Ozarks hills:

As darkness came the woods grew wilder. The heaped rocks with twisted roots of trees made strange figures. I seemed to see primeval shapes with slanting foreheads, deep arched necks, and heaping shoulders playing on primordial flutes. I had a sort of cloudy vision of pictures I was to make long afterwards—a great female figure loomed out of the rocks holding mankind on her vast bosom. That night there came to me the title of the unborn picture, "The Nursing Monster." (*Story* 57–58)

As with the Kewpie, so with her Monster. Both were conceived in the Ozarks hills, having "come up from sleep, where the truth lies."[22]

---

[22] We take this last phrase from O'Neill's Washington Square notebook.

Let us thank those who have assisted with this essay. At the head of the list stands David O'Neill, Roses's grand-nephew, who gave free access to his collection of O'Neilliana. All the artwork and diary entries reproduced here are taken from his collection. We thank the staff of Meyer Library Special Collections and Archives at Missouri State University for temporarily housing these materials for facilitating their reproduction. And we thank photographer Jimmie Allen, Assistant Professor of Art and Design at Missouri State University, for reproducing several of the larger pieces featured in this essay.

Works Cited

Baumlin, James S., and Lanette Cadle. "Portraits of Womanhood in the Artwork of Rose O'Neill." *Moon City Review 2009: An Annual of Poetry, Story, Art, and Criticism.* Ed. Jane Hoogestraat and Lanette Cadle. Springfield, MO: Moon City, 2009. 190-225. Print.

Baumlin, James S., Tita French Baumlin, and George H. Jensen, eds. *Post-Jungian Criticism: Theory and Practice.* Albany, NY: The State U of New York P, 2004. Print.

Brown. Edythe. H. "Rose O'Neill's Sculptured Drawings." *International Studio* (March, 1922): 63-68. Print.

Gibran, Kahlil. *Sea and Foam: A Book of Aphorisms.* New York: Knopf, 1926. Print.

Jung, Carl G. *The Collected Works of C. G. Jung.* Ed. Sir Herbert Read, Michael Fordham, and Gerhard Adler. Trans. R. F. C. Hull. 20 vols. Princton: Princeton UP, 1953-1977. Print.

Kindelien, Carlin T. "Rose O'Neill." *Notable American Women: A Biographical Dictionary.* Vol. 2. Ed. Edward T. James. Cambridge, MA: Belknap, 1971. 650-51. Print.

Kirkendall, Shellie, and Bob Haas, eds. *Rose O'Neill's Sweet Monsters.* Mira Loma, CA: Q.P. Publishing, n.d. Print.

Long, Haniel. "The Professor of Dreams." *Century Magazine* 104.3 (July 1922): 354-61. Print.

———. *Notes for a New Mythology.* 1926. New York: Johnson Reprints, 1971. Print.

O'Neill. Rose. *Garda.* New York: Doubleday, 1929. Print.

———. *The Master-Mistress: Poems, with Drawings by the Author.* New York: Knopf, 1922. Print.

———. *The Story of Rose O'Neill: An Autobiography.* Ed. Miriam Formanek-Brunell. Columbia: U of Missouri P, 1997. Print.

Sharp, Daryl. *Jung Lexicon: A Primer of Terms and Concepts.* Toronto: Inner City, 1991. Web version: <http://www.psychceu.com/Jung/sharplexicon.html>. 14 July 2010.

Ulanov, Ann Belford. *The Feminine in Jungian Psychology and in Christian Theology*. Evanston: Northwestern UP, 1971. Print.

Young-Eisendrath, Polly. "Gender and Contrasexuality: Jung's Contribution and Beyond." *The Cambridge Companion to Jung*. Ed. Polly Young-Eisendrath and Terence Dawson. Cambridge: Cambridge UP, 1997. 223-29. Print.

Notes on Contributors

Seno Gumira Ajidarma (b. June 19, 1958) is an award-winning Indonesian short story writer, scriptwriter, essayist, and journalist who has published more than 25 books, including *Negeri Senja* (*The Sunset Land*) and *Sepotong Senja Untuk Pacarku* (*A Slice of Sunset for My Sweetheart*). He won the 1997 SEA Write Award (Southeast Asian Writers Award) and Khatulistiwa Literary Awards for both 2004 and 2005. *Eyewitness*, an English translation of his work by Jan Lingard, won the (Australian) Dinny O'Hearn Prize for Literary Translation in 1997.

Naoko Awa (1943–1993) was born in Tokyo and while growing up lived in different parts of Japan. As a child, she read fairy tales by the Brothers Grimm, Hans Christian Andersen, and Wilhelm Hauff, as well as *The Arabian Nights*. Her books have been translated into Chinese, Korean, and French. Her first collection in English, *The Fox's Window and Other Stories*, will be published in 2010.

James S. Baumlin teaches English at Missouri State. He has published widely in fields of criticism, the history of rhetoric, and English renaissance poetry.

Gemma Bellhouse is completing her BA in English at Missouri State University. She plans on graduate school in linguistics and a career in ESL.

Ben Bogart is a recent graduate of Missouri State University, earning an MA in English for his studies in Creative Writing. He currently lives in Springfield, Missouri with his wife Gina.

Per Aage Brandt, Danish poet, was born in Buenos Aires in 1944. He received his MA degree from the University of Copenhagen and his PhD from the Sorbonne, his main areas of training being Romance Philology, Linguistics, and Comparative Literature. He is currently the Emile B. de Sauzé Professor and Chair of the Department of Modern Languages at Case Western Reserve University. He has published close to thirty volumes of poetry while also publishing extensively in the fields of semiotics, linguistics, poetics, literary criticism, and aesthetics.

Lanette Cadle is an Associate Professor at Missouri State who teaches both rhetoric/ composition and poetry. Her poems have appeared in *Crab Orchard Review* and *Connecticut Review*.

235

MARCUS CAFAGÑA is the author of two books of poetry, *The Broken World* and *Roman Fever*. His poems have also appeared in *Ploughshares*, *Poetry*, and *The Southern Review*. He coordinates the creative writing program at Missouri State.

TED CHILES' stories have appeared or are forthcoming in several literary journals including *Vestal Review*, *The Anemone Sidecar*, *seven letter words quarterly*, *Waccamaw*, and *The Abacot Journal*. Living in Santa Barbara, California, with a poet and three cats, Chiles teaches Economics, the most dramatic of the Social Sciences.

JIM DANIELS' forthcoming books include *Having a Little Talk with Capital P Poetry*, Carnegie Mellon University Press, and *From Milltown to Malltown*, a collaborative book with photographer Charlee Brodsky and writer Jane McCafferty, Marick Press.

LANDIS DUFFETT is an itinerant scholar and teacher of the humanities. He was born in Lexington, Missouri, and currently resides in Amherst, Massachusetts.

PETE DUVAL is the fiction editor of *Dogwood: A Journal of Poetry & Prose* and the technical editor of the online women's poetry journal *Mezzo Cammin*. His story collection *Rear View* won the Bread Loaf Writers' Conference Bakeless Prize for Fiction, the Connecticut Book Award for Fiction, and was a finalist for the Los Angeles Times Art Seidenbaum Award for First Fiction. He has new work appearing in *Alaska Quarterly Review* and *Witness*. Duval teaches at West Chester University and lives in Philadelphia's Chinatown.

JAMIE FRUSH is a Missouri native, currently residing in San Francisco. "Dear Refugee" was inspired after reading Mahmoud Darwish's *Memory for Forgetfulness*.

JEANNINE HALL GAILEY'S first book of poetry, *Becoming the Villainess*, was published by Steel Toe Books. Poems from the book were featured on *The Writer's Almanac* and *Verse Daily*; two were included in 2007's *The Year's Best Fantasy and Horror*. She volunteers with *Crab Creek Review* and teaches at National University's MFA program.

D. GILSON is an MFA candidate in creative nonfiction and poetry at Chatham University. A native of the Ozark Mountain region, he is particularly interested in outsider status in such a place; his work explores this theme, focusing particularly on issues of queerness and masculinity. His work has appeared in *The New York Quarterly*, *Elder Mountain*, *OzarksWatch*, and *Iezine*.

NANCY GOLD is living in Ann Arbor, where she refuses to age gracefully.

ALYSSE HOTZ is a second-year MFA student at the University of Missouri-Kansas City, where she holds the Stanley H. Durwood Fellowship for creative writing. Her poems have appeared in *Origami Condom*, *Rougarou*, *Porchlight*, and are forthcoming in the *San Pedro River Review*, *The Driftwood Review*, and *Other Poetry*.

REBECCA JAMES holds an MFA from Queens University and teaches English at South Piedmont Community College. Her poetry has appeared in several journals including *Margie*.

TOSHIYA KAMEI received the Spanish Ministry of Culture Translation Grant for his translation of Espido Freire's *Irlanda* (FTR Press, forthcoming). His other translations have appeared in *The Global Game* (University of Nebraska Press, 2008), *Sudden Fiction Latino* (W. W. Norton, 2010), and *My Mother She Killed Me, My Father He Ate Me* (Penguin Books, 2010).

HERNÁN MIGOYA is an author of novels, short stories, biographies, and comic books, as well as a director and writer of screenplay. *Putas es poco* is a continuation of an earlier collection of short stories, *Todas putas*.

TONI MITCHELL is a Creative Writing student at Missouri State University. Her fiction has previously been published in the Crowder *Quill*.

ERIC MORROW is currently an undergraduate at Missouri State University. His field of study is Secondary Education and hopes to be teaching High School Speech, Theatre, and English courses within a year.

ERIC PERVUKHIN, Professor in Art and Design at Missouri State, is internationally recognized for his work as a painter, printmaker, photographer, and designer.

JULIE PLATT is the author of the poetry chapbooks *In the Kingdom of My Familiar* (Tilt Press, 2008) and *Imitation Animals* (Gold Wake Press, 2009); her poems have appeared in such journals as *The Laurel Review*, *Bellingham Review*, and *Hayden's Ferry Review*, and her work is featured in *Dzanc Books Best of the Web 2010* anthology. She studies digital rhetoric and teaches writing at Michigan State University.

KIM STANLEY ROBINSON is best known for his *Mars* series, excerpted here as a companion piece to "Martian Justice: A Student's Recollections of Dr. William J. Burling." Writing literary science fiction, he is the recipient of the Hugo, Nebula, and Locus Awards.

THOM SATTERLEE'S first book translation, *The Hangman's Lament: Poems of Henrik Nordbrandt*, received the American-Scandinavian Foundation Translation Prize. His *These Hands: Selected Poetry of Per Aage Brandt* is scheduled for publication in 2010. His book of original poems, *Burning Wyclif*, received the Walt McDonald First-Book in Poetry Prize, was named an American Library Association Notable Book, and was a finalist for the *L.A. Times* Book Award in poetry. Satterlee teaches creative writing and is Program Director for the Center for the Study of C. S. Lewis & Friends at Taylor University in Upland, Indiana. He is completing a second book of poetry with support from an NEA grant.

NIKKI SETTELMEYER is a creative writer and translator at the University of Arkansas. Her fiction and poetry have been published in *North Country* and *Art Amiss*. She has won the Katherine Anne Porter, Katherine B. Tiffany, Boen Fiction, and Lily Peter awards for her fiction writing. This is her first translation publication.

MARIE SCHURK is a 2009 graduate of Missouri State University where she earned a bachelor's degree in Communication and a minor in Creative Writing.

J. M. SHIVELEY is the editor of *HIVE: A Somewhat Quarterly Comics* journal which is published through the mini comic D.I.Y. group Grimalkin Press. He also loves to hear from readers and talk about really nerdy things like pen cartridge to well ink conversion schematics and golems.

KINSLEY STOCUM is currently a creative writing major at Missouri State. This is her first publication.

JUNED SUBHAN is a former graduate of Glasgow University who has had work published in various journals including *Ontario Review, Cimarron Review, Indiana Review* and *North American Review*.

LIAM R. WATTS has Theatre and English BAs from MSSU and is currently completing his first novel and Master's thesis in English at Missouri State. He then plans on pursuing a PhD in posthuman cultural criticism.

MARK WISNIEWSKI is the author of the novel *Confessions of a Polish Used Car Salesman,* the collection of stories *All Weekend With the Lights On,* and the book of poems *One of Us One Night.* He's won a Pushcart Prize and work of his appeared in *Best American Short Stories 2008.* Poems of his formerly in print appear in "Poem of the Week" on markwisniewski. blogspot.com.

CHAD WOODY bachelored at Missouri State and mastered at UF Gainesville. His publications include *The Iowa Review, Mid-American Review, Forge,* and others. Springfield's *Good Girl Art Gallery* continues to host his lavish displays of eyestrain-inducing minor works. He and Heather Johansen just celebrated their wooden anniversary.

SARAH WYNN is a recent MA graduate from Missouri State pursuing a doctorate at the University of Mississippi. She is currently working on a science fiction novel that includes poetic sequences.

WAWAN EKO YULIANTO is a Master's student in the Program in Comparative Literature and Cultural Studies, University of Arkansas, Fayetteville, where he is concentrating on literary translation (translating mostly the short stories of Indonesian author Seno Gumira Ajidarma) and American Literature. His translation of Azadeh Moaveni's memoir, *Lipstick Jihad,* was published by Banana Publisher in 2007.

Moon City Press is a joint venture of the Missouri State University
Departments of English and Art and Design.
With series lists in "Arts and Letters" and
"Ozarks History and Culture,"
Moon City Press
features collaborations
between students and faculty
over the various aspects of publication:
research, writing, editing, layout and design.